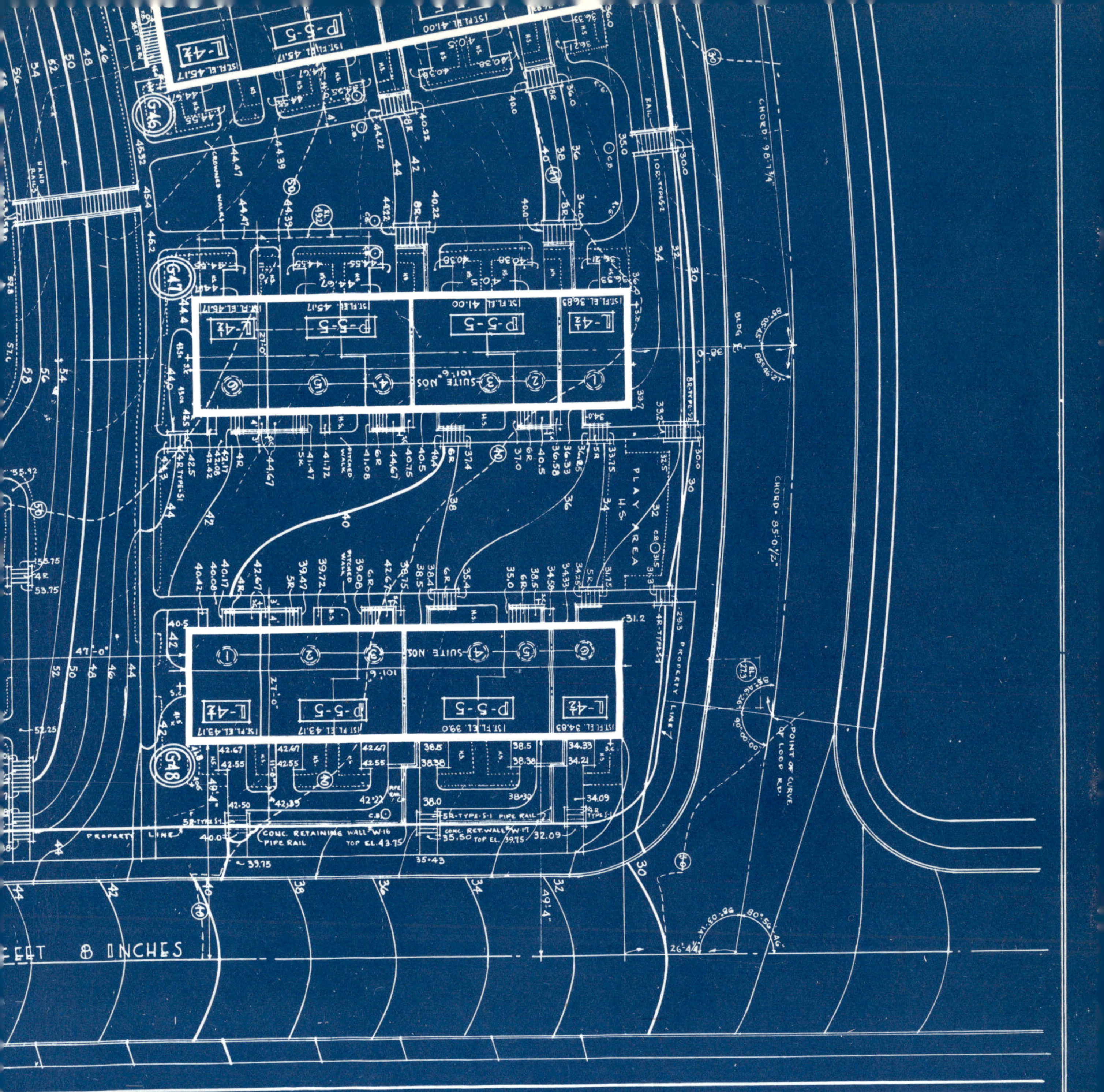

An Economic Analysis of The Housing and Urban Development Act of 1968

by ROBERT P. O'BLOCK
with ROBERT H. KUEHN, Jr.

AN ECONOMIC ANALYSIS OF THE HOUSING AND URBAN DEVELOPMENT ACT OF 1968

An Economic Analysis of
The Housing and Urban Development Act of 1968

BY ROBERT P. O'BLOCK
WITH ROBERT H. KUEHN, JR.
Formerly Research Associates in Business Administration
Harvard University

DIVISION OF RESEARCH
GRADUATE SCHOOL OF BUSINESS ADMINISTRATION
HARVARD UNIVERSITY

Boston · 1970

Library of Congress Catalog Card No. 73–108573
ISBN 0–87584–084–1

Faculty research at the Harvard Business School is undertaken with the expectation of publication. In such publication the authors responsible for the research project are also responsible for statements of fact, opinions, and conclusions expressed. Neither the Harvard Business School, its Faculty as a whole, nor the President and Fellows of Harvard College reach conclusions or make recommendations as results of Faculty research.

PRINTED IN THE UNITED STATES OF AMERICA

Foreword

The Urban Analysis Project at the Harvard Business School began in January 1968 as "a comprehensive research program in the application of modern business management methods to the problems of urban planning and administration." Under the direction of Maurice D. Kilbridge, then Professor of Business Administration and now Dean of the Harvard Graduate School of Design, the Project has been "based on the belief that the concepts and methods of management science developed in business administration can be applied to many urban problems." Over the last two years a number of such applications have been developed, including: a conceptual framework for urban planning models; an analysis of the role of models in urban planning; a survey of urban management information systems; an economic model for low-cost housing; an informational system for social indicators; an analysis of functional districts in the urban system; and a model for branch bank location. These applications have been published as working papers and several will be expanded in a forthcoming book entitled *Urban Analysis* (to be published by the Harvard Business School's Division of Research later this year).

The present work, by Robert P. O'Block and Robert H. Kuehn, Jr., Research Associates in Business Administration, is one of the most interesting and timely products of the Urban Analysis Project. It represents the first use of a computer model for systematic analysis of housing subsidy and cost alternatives. It also provides basic information needed by decision makers to assess the impact of alternative public policies and housing industry activities.

The major support for the Urban Analysis Project and for this study has come from an allocation of funds from gifts to the School by The Associates of the Harvard Business School. As always, our thanks go to these Associates for their continuing support of the School's research program. Additional support for Mr. O'Block's research came from the Harvard University Program on Technology and Society, for which we are very appreciative.

LAWRENCE E. FOURAKER
Dean

Soldiers Field
Boston, Massachusetts
March 1970

Preface

This study is a product of the Urban Analysis Project of the Harvard Business School's Division of Research and fulfills part of the project's general purpose, which is to apply management science methods in the analysis of urban problems.

Project participants very early identified housing economics as an area where these methods of quantitative analysis seemed particularly applicable. A few of the computer models which resulted from this analysis are applied in this study to the Housing and Urban Development Act of 1968. This legislation reaffirmed the goal of a "decent home and suitable living environment for every American family," and asked that this goal be "substantially achieved within the next decade by the construction or rehabilitation of 26 million housing units, 6 million of these for low and moderate income families." Toward this end the Act established several new programs for subsidizing construction or rehabilitation of low-income housing. Our analysis projects the total number of new and rehabilitated housing units that potentially could be provided under various levels of government funding for each program. Although numerous provisions of the Act have been modified since this study was completed, e.g., income and mortgage limits, interest rate ceilings, and so on, the developed methodology and conclusions still hold.

Many persons not listed as the authors of this monograph contributed importantly to its completion. Particular thanks are due Professor Richard Rosenbloom, a member of the Harvard Business School Faculty and an Associate of the Harvard University Program on Technology and Society, for conceiving the idea of the housing model and the use of computers in housing finance. Thomas Seessel and Ralph Brown, Executive Director and Director of Policy and Programs, respectively, of the New Jersey Housing Finance Agency, helped develop and field test these ideas. Professor John Collins of the Alfred P. Sloan School of Management of the Massachusetts Institute of Technology first suggested that our housing analysis techniques be applied to the 1968 Housing Act, and he contributed much helpful advice during the course of the project. David Sloan of the Harvard Law School, along with Robert Huefner and Paul Teplitz of the Harvard Business School, helped organize the study and read various drafts of the manuscript. Charles Fager of Harvard Divinity School, our very capable editor, shepherded the manuscript down a long and complicated path from the authors to the publisher, ably assisted by Mrs. Rose Jevelekian, our indefatigable typist.

Maurice D. Kilbridge
Robert P. O'Block
Robert H. Kuehn, Jr.

Table of Contents

Chapter One: Introduction and Conclusions 1
- Why the Low-Income Housing Shortage? 1
- A Summary of Conclusions 2
  - Base Cases (BCs) 2
  - Profitability 2
  - BC Variations 3
  - Section 236 3
  - Section 236 Projections 3
  - Section 236 Variations 3
  - Section 235 3
  - Section 221(h) 4
  - Rent Supplement 4
  - Public Housing 4
  - Section 506 4

Chapter Two: The Housing Analyzer 6
- Need for a Housing Model 6
- Basic Principle of the Model 6
- Planning and Construction Costs 7
- Operating Expenses 7
- The Cost Data Bank 7
- The Tenants' Ability to Pay 7
- Cash Flows over the Project Life 8
- The Computer Program 9
- The Profitability Subroutines 9
- The Housing Analyzer in Use 10

Chapter Three: Analysis and Interpretation 12
- Base Cases 12
  - BC Projects 12
  - Profitability Analysis 14
  - BC Variations 18
- Section 236 Program 23
  - Section 236 24
  - Section 236 Three-Year Projections 26
  - Selected Cost Variations 28
  - Summary 31
- Other Subsidy Programs 32
  - Section 235 Program 35
  - Section 221(h) Program 36
  - Rent Supplement Program 36
  - Public Housing 37
  - Section 506 Program 37
  - Summary 38
- Recapitulation 39

Appendix: Procedure and Detailed Results 41
Base Cases and Profitability Analysis 41
Steps 1 and 3: Base Cases 41
Steps 2 and 4: Variable Testing for Nonprofit Base Cases . . . 54
Section 236 Program 64
Steps 5 and 6: Section 236 Program Applied to Nonprofit Base Cases 64
Step 7: Section 236 Program Applied to a Nonprofit Base Cases Mix 65
Steps 8 and 9: Section 236 Program Applied to Limited-Dividend Base Cases 65
Step 10: Section 236 Program Applied to New Construction and Rehabilitation Base Cases with a Mix of Sponsorship 67
Steps 11 and 12: Variable Testing for Section 236 Program Applied to Nonprofit Base Cases 69
Other Subsidy Programs 73
Step 13: Section 235 Program Applied to Special New Construction and Rehabilitation Base Cases 73
Step 14: Section 221(h) Program Applied to Nonprofit Rehabilitation Base Case 75
Step 15: Rent Supplement Program Applied to Nonprofit New Construction and Rehabilitation Base Cases 76
Step 16: Public Housing Program Applied to Nonprofit New Construction and Rehabilitation Base Cases 77
Step 17: Section 506 Program Applied to Nonprofit New Construction and Rehabilitation Base Cases 78
Bibliography 79

List of Tables

I Market Rents and Income Levels for Alternative Base Cases 12
II Per Unit Cost Categories for Alternative Base Cases 13
III Effect on Market Rents and Income Levels of Selected Cost Variables: New Construction and Rehabilitation, Nonprofit 20
IV Relative Effectiveness of Alternative $100,000 Subsidies: New Construction and Rehabilitation, Nonprofit 22
V Section 236 Rents and Income Levels for Alternative Base Cases 24
VI Effect of Section 236 Appropriations on the Number of Units Provided, Applied to Alternative Base Cases 25
VII Effect of Selected Cost Variations on Section 236 Rents and Income Levels: New Construction and Rehabilitation, Nonprofit 29
VIII Effect of Section 236 Appropriations on Number of Units Provided with Selected Cost Variations: New Construction and Rehabilitation . . . 29
IX Rents and Income Levels for Other Subsidy Programs: New Construction and Rehabilitation, Nonprofit 34
X Effect of Appropriations on the Number of Units Provided by Other Subsidy Programs: New Construction and Rehabilitation, Nonprofit 34
A–1 Interest and Amortization: New Construction, Limited-Dividend 50
A–2 Depreciation: New Construction, Limited-Dividend 51
A–3 Cash Flows: New Construction, Limited-Dividend 52
A–4 Capital Gains Profits: New Construction, Limited-Dividend 53
A–5 Profitability and Present Value: New Construction, Limited-Dividend . . . 54
A–6 Land Costs: New Construction and Rehabilitation, Nonprofit 55
A–7 Construction and Rehabilitation Costs: New Construction and Rehabilitation, Nonprofit 56
A–8 Interest Rates: New Construction and Rehabilitation, Nonprofit 58
A–9 Mortgage Terms: New Construction and Rehabilitation, Nonprofit 59
A–10 Operating Expenses: New Construction and Rehabilitation, Nonprofit . . . 61
A–11 Percentage of Family Income Spent for Rent: New Construction and Rehabilitation, Nonprofit 63
A–12 Real Estate Taxes (Gross-Shelter-Rent Method): New Construction and Rehabilitation, Nonprofit 64
A–13 Section 236 Basic Rents and Income Levels: New Construction and Rehabilitation, Nonprofit 64
A–14 Section 236 Basic Rents and Income Levels: New Construction and Rehabilitation, Limited-Dividend 66
A–15 Section 236 Unit Distribution: New Construction and Rehabilitation, Nonprofit 68
A–16 Section 236 Operating Expenses: New Construction and Rehabilitation, Nonprofit 68
A–17 Section 236 Interest Rate Changes: New Construction and Rehabilitation, Nonprofit 68

A–18 Percentage of Income Spent for Section 236 Rent: New Construction and Rehabilitation, Nonprofit 69
A–19 Section 236 Construction and Rehabilitation Costs: New Construction and Rehabilitation, Nonprofit 69
A–20 Section 235 Basic Rents and Income Levels per Year: New Construction and Rehabilitation, Nonprofit 74
A–21 Section 221(h) Basic Rents and Income Levels: Rehabilitation, Nonprofit . . 75
A–22 Rent Supplement Basic Rents and Income Levels: New Construction and Rehabilitation, Nonprofit 76
A–23 Public Housing Basic Rents and Income Levels: New Construction and Rehabilitation, Nonprofit 77
A–24 Section 506 Basic Rents and Income Levels: New Construction and Rehabilitation, Nonprofit 78

List of Illustrations

Diagrams

A Principle of the Housing Analyzer Model 7
B Housing Project Cash Flows 8
C General Flow Diagram of Housing Analyzer Model 9
D Flow Diagram of Profitability Subroutine 10
E Section 236 Subsidy Formula 23
F Section 235 Subsidy Formula 32
G Section 221(h) Subsidy Formula 32
H Rent Supplement Subsidy Formula 33
I Public Housing Subsidy Formula 33
J Section 506 Subsidy Formula 33
K Cost Structure, New Construction and Rehabilitation, Nonprofit 42

Graphs

1 Economist's View of the Low-Income Housing Market 1
2 Past and Projected Housing Production: 1958–1978 2
3 Tax Position vs. Years of Holding: New Construction, Limited-Dividend . . 15
4 Profit Position vs. Year of Holding or Sale: New Construction, Limited-Dividend 16
5 Profitability Criteria vs. Year of Holding or Sale: New Construction, Limited-Dividend 18
6 Present Value vs. Year of Holding or Sale: New Construction, Limited-Dividend 18
7 Changes in Average Rent vs. Changes in Selected Cost Variables: New Construction, Nonprofit 21
8 Changes in Average Rent vs. Changes in Selected Cost Variables: Rehabilitation, Nonprofit 21
9 Annual Section 236 Appropriations vs. Number of Units Provided: Alternative Sponsorship 25
10 Annual Section 236 Appropriations vs. Number of Units Provided: New Construction and Rehabilitation, Nonprofit 25
11 Annual Appropriations for Other Subsidy Programs vs. Number of Units Provided: New Construction, Nonprofit 35

12 Annual Appropriations for Other Subsidy Programs vs. Number of Units Provided: Rehabilitation, Nonprofit 35
13 Number of Units Provided under Other Subsidy Programs (and Section 236 Program) vs. Rentals Required and Income Levels Served: By Program 38
14 Number of Units Provided under Other Subsidy Programs (and Section 236 Program) vs. Rentals Required and Income Levels Served: Total . . . 38
A–1 Change in Average Rent vs. Change in Land and Building Acquisition Costs: New Construction and Rehabilitation, Nonprofit 53
A–2 Change in Average Rent vs. Change in Construction Cost: New Construction and Rehabilitation, Nonprofit 57
A–3 Change in Average Rent vs. Change in Interest Rate: New Construction and Rehabilitation, Nonprofit 57
A–4 Change in Average Rent vs. Change in Mortgage Term: New Construction, Nonprofit 60
A–5 Change in Average Rent vs. Change in Mortgage Term: Rehabilitation, Nonprofit 60
A–6 Change in Average Rent vs. Change in Operating Expenses: New Construction and Rehabilitation, Nonprofit 62
A–7 Annual Section 236 Appropriations vs. Number of Units Provided: New Construction and Rehabilitation, Nonprofit 65
A–8 Annual Section 236 Appropriations vs. Number of Units Provided: New Construction, Rehabilitation, and Mixed, Nonprofit 65
A–9 Annual Section 236 Appropriations vs. Number of Units Provided: New Construction and Rehabilitation, Limited-Dividend 66
A–10 Annual Section 236 Appropriations vs. Number of Units Provided: New Construction, Mixed Sponsorship 67
A–11 Annual Section 236 Appropriations vs. Number of Units Provided: Rehabilitation, Mixed Sponsorship 67
A–12 Annual Section 235 Appropriations vs. Number of Units Provided: New Construction and Rehabilitation, Nonprofit 74
A–13 Annual Section 221(h) Appropriations vs. Number of Units Provided: Rehabilitation, Nonprofit 75
A–14 Annual Rent Supplement Appropriations vs. Number of Units Provided: New Construction and Rehabilitation, Nonprofit. 76
A–15 Annual Public Housing Appropriations vs. Number of Units Provided: New Construction and Rehabilitation, Nonprofit. 78
A–16 Annual Section 506 Appropriations vs. Number of New Units Provided: New Construction and Rehabilitation, Nonprofit. 78

Exhibits

1 Cost Variables, Assumptions, and Estimates: New Construction and Rehabilitation, Nonprofit 42–45
2 Cost Variables, Assumptions, and Estimates: New Construction and Rehabilitation, Limited-Dividend 47–49

Chapter One

INTRODUCTION AND CONCLUSIONS

Why the Low-Income Housing Shortage?

The national shortage of low-income housing is not due to some mysterious malfunctioning of the housing market. Certainly there are distortions in the market caused by racial discrimination and other external influences, but as a mechanism for equating supply and demand the market is working about as it should. The trouble is that housing suppliers simply find it impossible to reduce costs enough to place satisfactory housing within the reach of lower income families while making such housing a profitable investment.

Suppose the cost of a reasonably adequate apartment house of two-bedroom units is $14,000 per unit (about the national average for standard low-cost housing) and annual operating expenses are $450 per unit (also about average). Assuming a 5% interest rate and a 40-year term, the annual level payment required to pay both interest and principal comes to about $816 per unit per year, which when added to the $450 operating cost totals $1,266 per year. In other words, these costs require a rent, without any profit to the owner, of about $105 per unit per month. If the family budget allots one-quarter of income for rent (a norm frequently used in planning because it is thought to fit the American expenditure pattern), then the family wishing to occupy these units must have take-home pay of at least $5,000 per year. But by U.S. Census Bureau estimates, in 1966 there were about 15 million families in the United States with incomes less than this. These families either were paying more than a quarter of their income for rent and skimping on food or other necessities, or living in crowded or substandard housing, or some equally undesirable combination of these.

Given our national income distribution, building and operating costs, and alternative investment opportunities, the market cannot satisfy the demand for low-income housing without some form of direct or indirect subsidy. The profit is simply not there. Economic realities prohibit the attainment of desired social goals. (See Graph 1.)

Graph 1. Economist's View of the Low-Income Housing Market

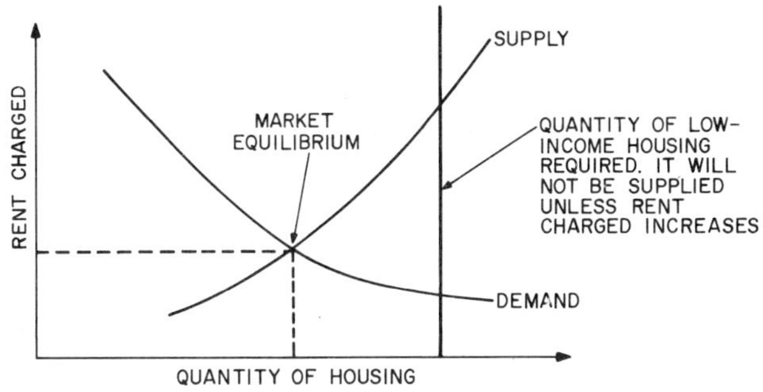

Note: The demand curve represents different quantities of housing that people will—at any time and with other things held equal—rent at each different price. The supply curve represents the relationship between rent charged and the quantity of housing that builders will produce, all other things being equal. Market equilibrium occurs only at a price where the quantities supplied and demanded are equal. At a price higher than the equilibrium intersection of the supply and demand curves, the amount builders will continue to supply will exceed the quantity consumers will demand; downward pressure on rents will result as some builders undermine the going rent. At prices lower than the equilibrium intersection, builders will stop supplying the market for lack of adequate profit incentive and consumer demand pressure will bid up rents.

The Report of the President's Committee on Urban Housing estimates that: "About 7.8 million American families—one in every eight—cannot now afford to pay the market price for standard housing costing no more than 20% of their total income." To satisfy this demand the Committee urges production of "2.6 million units annually, compared to the current rate of 1.5 million new housing starts per year." It further recommends full and imaginative use of federal subsidy programs to bring this housing within a price range lower-income families can afford. (See Graph 2.)

To help achieve these goals—which by now, with minor variations in the numbers, have become national goals—the 90th Congress passed the Housing and Urban Development Act of 1968 (HUDA 68), by far the most comprehensive housing legislation yet passed in our country. It contains several programs for subsidizing construction and rehabilitation of low-income housing for both rental and ownership. Although time and experience alone can tell how useful these programs will be in meeting the nation's housing goals, the need to plan ahead requires that estimates be made of their potential effectiveness.

Achievement of these goals does not, of course, depend on government subsidies alone, and the following analysis is not meant to imply that, given the assumed subsidy levels, low-income housing will automatically be built. A host of economic, organizational, institutional, and technological preconditions must first be met. Federal subsidy is one of these, necessary but not sufficient.

GRAPH 2. PAST AND PROJECTED HOUSING PRODUCTION: 1958–1978

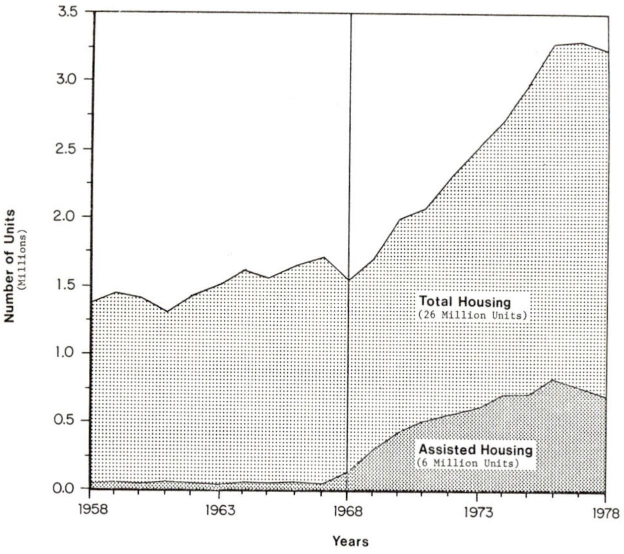

SOURCE: E. E. Kaiser, *A Decent Home: A Report of the President's Committee on Urban Housing, 1968.*

This study analyzes HUDA 68, projecting the Act's potential impact as measured by the number of low-income housing units possible with various amounts of federal expenditure, rents that must be charged for these units, and income levels of families the units will serve. The analysis has been made with the assistance of the Housing Analyzer Model (HAM) which is described in Chapter Two, a computer simulation model that generates the economic consequences of alternative subsidy programs, project types, profitability requirements, and other essential cost variables, assumptions, and estimates.

The study also provides basic information needed by decision makers to assess the impact of alternative public policies and private sector activities. Government policy issues include housing appropriations to be authorized and funded, the amount and type of subsidy to be provided, tax abatement, exemption and incentive policies, construction cost and interest rate ceilings to be imposed, federal funds to be allocated to research and development as against outright subsidy to tenants, and so forth. Business and economic issues include trends in construction labor and material costs, tax rates, alternative investment opportunities, technological breakthroughs, and so forth. For each policy alternative and set of economic forces, the decision maker requires basic data of the sort this report contains to arrive at an appropriate decision.

A SUMMARY OF CONCLUSIONS

Base Cases (BCs)

The four BC projects for new construction and rehabilitation serve as standards or bench marks against which changes in subsidy programs or appropriations, project composition or costs, and other variables can be tested. Rent and income levels resulting from the BC analyses clearly show that some form of subsidy will be essential to provide sufficient housing for low- and moderate-income families. The new construction (nonprofit) BC1 project contains 100 housing units at a cost of $22,000 per average unit. Market rentals range from $158 per month for a one-bedroom unit to $294 per month for a four-bedroom unit, an average of $227. Respective family income limits are $7,600, $14,100, and $10,900 per year. Type of sponsorship (nonprofit or limited-dividend) has little influence on market rents. The 100-unit rehabilitation (nonprofit) BC3 project costs $15,300 per average unit. Market rents average $173 per month, ranging from $120 for a one-bedroom unit to $223 for a four-bedroom unit. Respective income limits are $5,800, $10,755, and $8,300 per year, hardly "low-income" by any standards.

Profitability

This study employs four profit measures of the limited-dividend sponsor's return on equity: average after-tax, average cash flow, average after-tax + capital gains inflow, and average cash flow + capital gains inflow. The investment's net present values are calculated for each year the project is held and as if the project were sold in each year. Profitability varies widely depending on which index is used for evaluation and which year is considered. Before-tax income in a project's early years is negative due to large depreciation and interest deductions, yielding a negative after-tax income or tax savings. The yearly cash flow resulting from the limited-dividend distributions plus this tax savings is substantial. Capital gains inflow is a function of the holding period length, increasing in a project's later years as the recapture and other provisions of capital gains tax rules are relaxed. This type of profitability analysis allows the investor to assess options available as to depreciable life, depreciation methods, tax shelter, holding period, and so forth, and to make any beneficial adjustments. Programs designed to stimulate private investment through tax incentives should also consider these alternatives.

BC Variations

The impact of any cost variation on rents, incomes, and number of units constructed is a function of each project's internal cost structure. This study considers five cost categories: land costs, construction or rehabilitation costs, debt service (mortgage term and interest rate), operating expenses, and real estate taxes. The ratio of land to construction costs, the ratio of annual operating expenses to debt service charges, the construction loan amount, time for construction, and many similar internal cost relationships will influence the effect of absolute cost changes on rents. The most sensitive cost category, in terms of absolute and percentage rent reductions, is construction or rehabilitation cost, for both new construction and rehabilitation BCs. However, a 10% reduction in these costs reduces rents only 8% and 5.5% for new construction and rehabilitation respectively. Obviously we cannot rely on construction cost savings alone to reduce low-income housing cost significantly. Simultaneous cost savings in several categories—land, construction, interest rate, taxes, and operating expenses—could, however, significantly reduce rents and income levels served.

Section 236

The Section 236 Program should be quite effective in reducing rents, thereby assisting lower-income families otherwise unable to afford new or rehabilitated housing. For the new construction (nonprofit) BC, the average market rent of $227 per month is subsidized through a periodic payment equivalent to $87 per month, resulting in an average Section 236 basic rent of $140. The income level necessary to support this rent, based on 25% of family income, is reduced by 38.4%, from $10,900 to $6,700 per year. For the rehabilitation (nonprofit) BC, the periodic payment is equivalent to $60 per month, resulting in an average Section 236 basic rent of $113 per month. This reduces income level from $8,300 to $5,100 per year, still above that of the truly low-income family.

Section 236 Projections

The new and rehabilitated units possible with $25 million of Section 236 subsidy are 24,000 and 34,600, respectively. Unless appropriations authorized by HUDA 68 are substantially increased, Section 236 will not achieve the Act's outlined objectives. A studied allocation between new construction and rehabilitation must also be made. Considering standards, specifications, and economic life, the issue is whether to provide a greater number of rehabilitated units at lower rents and incomes or fewer new units at higher rents and incomes but with improved standards and longer life.

Section 236 Variations

Selected BC cost changes have the following effects under the Section 236 subsidy formula:

- construction or rehabilitation cost changes affect rents, income levels, and number of units provided; but as the Section 236 subsidy formula does not fully absorb their impact, rent differentials result from project cost changes.
- interest rate changes affect primarily the number of units provided; the subsidy formula absorbs almost all the effective interest rate differential, but the periodic payments are subsequently adjusted, which changes the number of units provided.
- operating expense changes affect only rents and incomes; the subsidy formula does not compensate for these changes, so there is no change in the number of units provided.
- changes in the percentage of income spent for rent influence the income sector the subsidy serves, rather than rents or the number of units provided.

Section 235

Assuming a $12,500 rehabilitated dwelling cost, the Section 235 (home ownership) subsidy formula reduced required mortgage payments 54.1% by providing a maximum periodic payment of $47 per month per average unit. On this basis, 17,283 units are possible with a $10 million appropriation, 22.6% more units than could be provided with an equal Section 236 appropriation. The government apparently anticipates absorbing additional occupancy expenses with the difference between the 20% of income spent for housing under Section 235 and the 25% spent under Section 236. Occupancy expenses, however, could equal the mortgage payment itself, depending on home location and the degree to which the owner can do his own maintenance and repairs. Thus the Section 235 Program may prove unrealistic unless other provisions are made.

Section 221(h)

The Section 221(h) subsidy formula applied to the rehabilitation BC reduces required basic rents by 54.1%, from $173 to $113 per month, based on a $60 monthly interest rate subsidy, the same amounts as for the Section 236 subsidy formula applied to the BC. Similarly, the units provided by a given appropriation are the same as for Section 236. However, the Section 221(h) Program is to be phased out gradually as the Section 236 Program becomes operational.

Rent Supplement

The Rent Supplement Program applied to the rehabilitation BC reduces rents from $173 to $52 per month, representing a $121 monthly subsidy, the maximum allowable supplement payment, calculated as 70% of market rents. Rent Supplement Program projections decrease markedly, 50.4% compared with Section 236 projections, in number of units provided for a given appropriation, due to the $121 per month subsidy amount, just over twice the Section 236 periodic payment amount. It would seem preferable to spread any available appropriation over more units by attaching rent supplements to other subsidy programs. For example, $25 monthly rents are possible using a combination of Rent Supplements and Section 236 subsidies.

Public Housing

The Public Housing subsidy formula applied to the rehabilitation BC reduces rents and incomes by 60.2%, considering both debt service subsidies and real estate tax and contingency allowance reductions, a decrease in rents from $173 to $69 per month, based on a total subsidy amount of $104 per month. The units provided under the Public Housing Program decreased 30.1% from Section 236 projections for a given appropriation, because the Public Housing Program subsidizes all debt service requirements, while the maximum Section 236 decrease is to a 1% rate.

Section 506

The Section 506 Program applied to the rehabilitation BC reduces rents by 10.9%, from $173 to $154 per month. The subsidy is in the form of a land write-down during the development term, reducing land and building acquisition costs from $2,000 to $1 per unit. For $10 million of Section 506 appropriations, 5,000 rehabilitated units can be provided, a decrease of 63.9% from Section 236 rehabilitation projections for the same appropriation. This reduction in the units provided results from the lump-sum payment required in a given year, instead of annualized subsidies over the project life. Land write-down subsidies are useful, however, as a supplementary program, especially in high land-value urban areas.

* * *

These conclusions, abstracted from the main report's detailed analysis, begin to outline a low-income housing assistance strategy under HUDA 68. Given the numerous subsidy programs and limited government expenditures, the question is which programs meet the requirements most effectively and how resources can best be allocated among them. This report measures the various subsidy programs' provisions in terms of rentals required and income levels served. Appropriations are translated into the number of units provided under respective subsidy formulas. Taken together, these results provide a means of assessing HUDA 68's impact on the low-income housing market. By comparing calculated rentals, income levels, and number of units to actual need and demand, the effectiveness of programs and appropriations in satisfying objectives becomes apparent. Subsequently, adjustments can be made in subsidy application or resource allocation to better meet low-income market requirements.

This study projects cost variations in housing production, financing, and operation, and calculates the effects of cost increases and inflation on cost savings and efficiencies. This provides additional dimensions to the basic considerations, and anticipates the probable cost variations' impact on the effectiveness of alternative subsidy programs and expenditures.

The results also provide technical support for analysis of many broad policy issues, such as new construction versus rehabilitation, nonprofit versus limited-dividend sponsorship, and similar trade-offs in project composition, cost, investment, and management. These are explicitly discussed. Implicitly discussed are such issues as tax incentives versus direct subsidy payments, the influence of fiscal and monetary policy on housing, and private versus public initiative. For each issue, cost to the tenant, government, and investor can be identified and calculated. Future studies should define these issues more precisely and analyze the economic and social implications of low-income housing. Only with the assistance of such analysis can HUDA 68's full potential be realized and can the nation finally achieve its elusive goal of "a decent home and a suitable living environment for every American family."

Chapter Two

THE HOUSING ANALYZER

Any thorough cost analysis of a residential construction project, especially if the discounted cash flow method is used, soon outruns the capacity of slide rule and desk calculator. Each discounted cash flow calculation requires hundreds of separate computations, and, to be done correctly, the process must be repeated again and again under varying assumptions about financing method, discount rate, depreciation method, and so forth. The private investor seeking a single common criterion for comparing housing investment alternatives under varying assumptions must simulate each alternative's cash flow characteristics. If he should also wish to vary his profitability measure, or consider systematically the element of uncertainty in future receipts or expenditures, the task becomes mechanically impossible.

The government official wishing to evaluate various possible housing subsidy programs is in much the same bind. He needs to know the effects on rent levels and investment return of various possible subsidy programs under a bewildering number of combinations of economic and technical assumptions much like those the private investor must make.

Need for a Housing Model

Considering the many housing program variables, it is extremely difficult to assess and compare alternative programs to stimulate investment in low-income housing. A computer model is needed that systematically analyzes the many alternative variable combinations and sorts out the most attractive. For private investors the model should be able to evaluate quickly and accurately a residential construction project's economic potential, or to find that combination of conditions and holding period length that will make it economically attractive. For the government policy maker the model should be able to test objectively and consistently the consequences of alternative plans and public programs. It would be nice if the model could include the social, psychological, and esthetic aspects of housing, but at this stage of our knowledge these qualitative and subjective variables are best left out of the calculation and judged separately.

Here are the kinds of questions the model should be able to answer:

- How do mortgage interest rates affect rents?
- How do land or building acquisition costs influence tax payments, interest payments, and rent levels?
- Which elements of construction, operating, and processing cost have the greatest impact on rents and profits?
- What is the most efficient way to subsidize low-income housing to get the greatest reduction in rents? And how does each form of subsidy affect investor profitability?
- Given a fixed budget for housing construction, what mix of housing types should a funding agency choose to achieve its objectives?

Basic Principle of the Model

The Housing Analyzer Model (HAM) presented here is a computer simulation program that serves both private investor and public policy maker equally well. It has been programmed for a time-sharing computer system and has been in use for several months in a large public agency.

HAM's organizing principle is shown in Diagram A. For a housing project to be economically feasible, interest and amortization costs associated with planning and construction, plus operating expenses, must be less than or equal to the aggregate rent or project income, which in turn must be less than or equal to the occupants' ability to pay. The model uses mathematical relationships to represent interactions between the diagram's four elements. These relationships include each major factor of cost and ability to pay. The model does not automatically provide the "one best" answer, but it generates the economic consequences of alternative assumptions about policies, programs, costs, and so forth, once these assumptions are spelled out and fed into it. The model's output provides the basis for judgment by the decision maker among alternative possibilities, and in this judgment he must weigh the social, political, and esthetic factors the model does not contain.

Planning and Construction Costs

As Diagram A shows, the model starts with planning and construction costs. Planning costs are the fees and entrepreneurial time spent in organizing the project. Land must be found and appraised, its physical characteristics investigated, and its legal status determined. Preliminary designs must be made. The approval of many government agencies—local, state, and sometimes federal—is usually required. Equity and loan capital must be found and financial terms arranged. Most of this work requires legal assistance. These planning costs are sunk in the project and have little salvage value if it does not get built.

water, and so forth), maintenance expenses (repairs, decorating, ground-keeping), janitorial wages, management fees, replacement reserves, and taxes. There is really very little systematic information available about these kinds of costs, yet they comprise a large part of the rent charged to tenants.

The Cost Data Bank

Work is under way on extension of a data bank to include important cost elements of constructing and operating several types of residential housing in various locations. One use of the data will be to test the sensitivity of all variables down stream in the model to various cost element changes. This kind of analysis will indicate the various cost elements' relative importance in determining rent levels and assist in sorting out controllable from uncontrollable costs.

DIAGRAM A

Principle of the Housing Analyzer Model

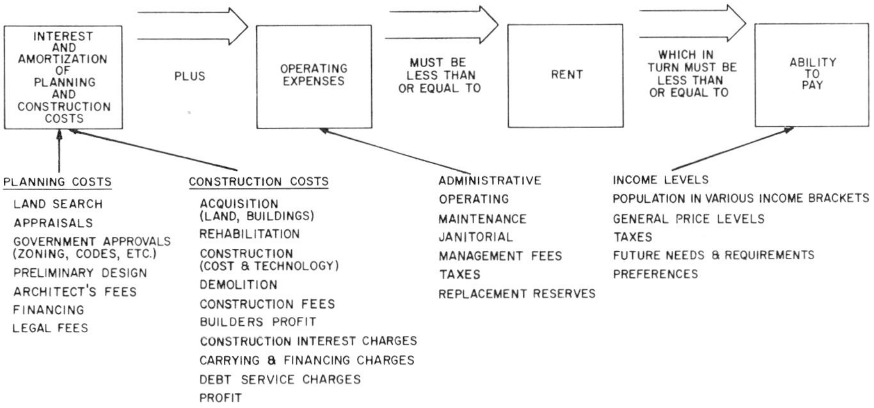

Construction costs include the acquisition cost of land and buildings, cost of either rehabilitation or new construction (which themselves depend on materials cost, wage levels, and available technology), construction fees, construction interest charges, and builder's profit. Planning and construction costs are summed to provide what is called the project's total replacement cost. Based on replacement cost, the investor's equity position, mortgage term, and interest rate combine to determine interest and amortization payments for the project's life.

Operating Expenses

Annual operating expenses, the second major cost category shown in Diagram A, consist of administrative costs, regular operating costs (fuel, electricity,

Another data bank use will be to compare cost elements among housing projects. One can ask the computer to find a similar project in a comparable location and to read out any element of cost desired, both in absolute terms and as a percentage of total replacement cost or annual operating cost.

The Tenants' Ability to Pay

As the diagram shows, construction and operating costs and profits determine the rent that must be charged, and, unless this rent is less than or equal to the tenants' ability to pay, the housing will remain vacant and more housing of its kind will not be built. The tenants' collective ability to pay rent, at any time and place, depends on patterns of family income and expenditure. To increase the supply of low-income housing provided by the private sector, profits must increase. This can be done by decreasing costs or increasing rents. With the housing industry's present structure and technology, and other impediments to cost reduction, significantly cheaper housing of the same standard is most unlikely. But if rents are increased the tenants will be unable to pay, resulting in overcrowding or other socially undesirable consequences. Some form of government subsidy is essential to satisfy both low-income tenants and investors.

Cash Flows Over the Project Life

HAM divides project life into three time periods: planning period, construction period, and mortgage period. Diagram B shows total and net cash flows for these periods for a new housing project. The vertical axis measures cash flows in or out (+ or −) and the horizontal axis measures time in the project life.

During the planning and construction periods, which for residential projects can vary in combined length from a few months to as long as eight to ten years, cash flows are all negative and costs tend to increase with time. Such increases spiral through the system to emerge in higher rents.

The mortgage period starts when construction is complete and extends over the repayment time of principal and interest of the original mortgage. During this period, interest and principal payments and operating expenses (including major repairs and replacements) are cash outflows and rents the cash inflow.[1] Interest and principal payments and depreciation are flows known with certainty, while the remaining flows are subject to unpredictable fluctuations. The model can analyze operating expenses and rents as fixed flows for the operating period life or they can be treated as uncertain.[2]

To have a positive net cash flow per year during the mortgage period, as depicted in Diagram B,

[1] When the project is sold, capital gains profit less taxes and repayment of mortgage principal represents another cash inflow.

[2] The uncertainty associated with occupancy levels, operating expenses, and rent payments serves as an example. At best, most projects can be characterized by subjective estimates of future cash flows, in terms of both level and variations. Most often the final decision to invest will depend upon the trade-off between expected profitability and the risk of project uncertainties.

DIAGRAM B

Housing Project Cash Flows

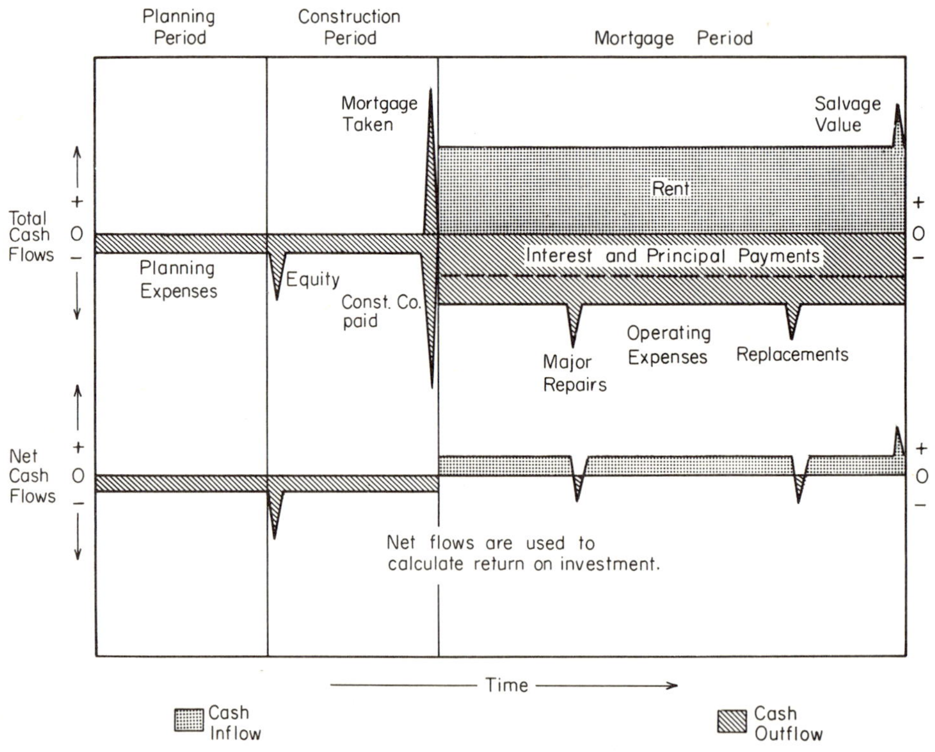

rental income must exceed the sum of yearly operating expenses and interest and principal payments. If this flow is negative, the project is not necessarily unprofitable for the owner. The project's net negative flows, calculated for income tax purposes (that is, adding in depreciation as an expense), can mean a tax savings for the investor, thus improving his overall (both housing projects and other ventures) cash picture. The higher his marginal tax bracket, the greater his savings. HAM is programmed to analyze both straight project cash flows and income tax flows, and to include capital gains inflows at the time of sale.

The Computer Program

The flow diagram of Diagram C shows HAM's computer program, instructions for which have been programmed in CAL (Computational All-Purpose Language) for the Harvard SDS 940 Time Sharing System. Once the project data are placed in file, Stage 1 of the program loads the program into memory and opens the specific data file to be analyzed.

Stage 2 estimates total cost of planning, organizing, and launching the project.

Stage 3 calculates land acquisition, land development, net demolition, and total structure costs for a project, cost categories provided as basic model input data.

Stage 4 uses the above results to calculate builder's general overhead, builder's profit, developer's profit, architect's fees, and so forth. These costs are usually a percentage of some or all the costs calculated in Stage 3. For example, the architect's rate usually is a percentage of land development plus structure costs plus builder's overhead and profit plus developer's profits.

Stage 5 employs a set of simultaneous equations to calculate total project replacement cost. (The Federal Housing Administration and other agencies use this figure to calculate the maximum mortgage allowable.)

Stage 6 determines fees and carrying charges based on total project replacement cost, ending a project's planning and construction period.

Stage 7 computes the maximum mortgage allowable for a project, as a function of the FHA, insurance company or bank percentage mortgage requirements, and the investor's desired equity position.

Stage 8 calculates mortgage interest and principal payments, taxes, and other operating expenses.

Stage 9 uses Stage 8's results to calculate the minimum rent per unit necessary to make the project economically sound. Profit, vacancy allowances, accessory income (parking lot rentals, coin machines, etc.), and management fees are taken into consideration.

Stage 10 prints out the information requested in Stage 1.

The print-out can be fitted to the user's specific desires and needs. The time-sharing system offers a flexible medium to furnish any output requested, provided of course that the information is or can be made available in the appropriate format.

The Profitability Subroutines

A set of HAM subroutines study the private investor's profit potential in building and operating housing projects. The subroutines are designed to analyze profitability by supplementing the construction and financing cost analysis presented in Stages 1 through 10 of the general routine shown in Diagram C. The Stage 10 outputs are inputs to Stages 11 through 15, shown in Diagram D. Given total replacement cost, mortgage principal, term and interest rate, investor's equity, and rent levels, this

DIAGRAM C

General Flow Diagram of Housing Analyzer Model

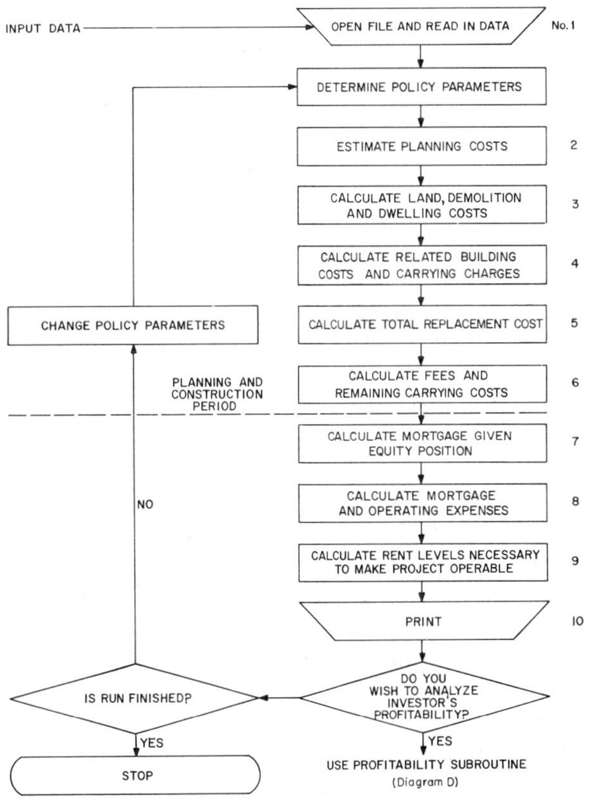

DIAGRAM D

FLOW DIAGRAM OF PROFITABILITY SUBROUTINE

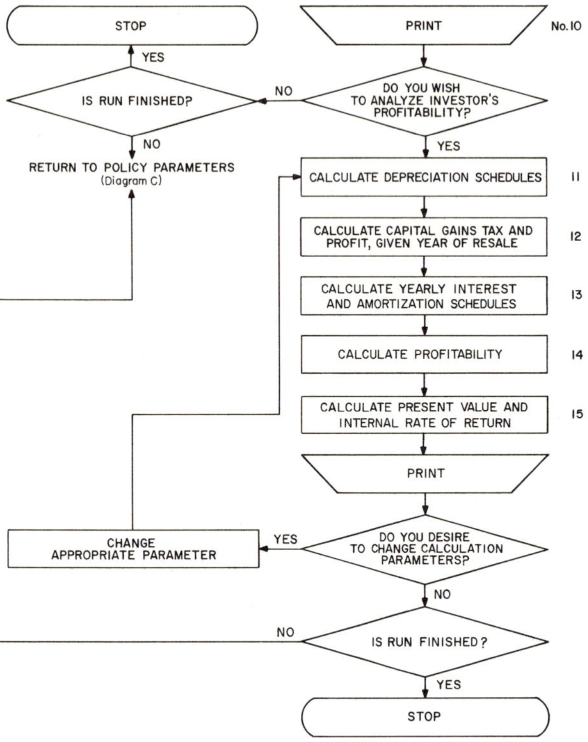

subroutine performs a systematic profitability analysis. One can, for example, run the subroutine for a given depreciation schedule, project holding period, tax rate, project selling price, discount rate, and so forth, and when the complete run has been made, one can cycle back, change any variable, and run again.

Stage 11 calculates annual depreciation expense and resulting undepreciated balance. One must select a depreciation method from among four approved types: straight-line, sum-of-years digits, 200% double-declining balance, and 150% double-declining balance. For tax purposes the difference between accelerated and straight-line depreciation is calculated and accumulated.

Stage 12 uses Stage 11's results to determine capital gains tax paid and profit received from outright sale of the project in any year. Tax and profit are a function of the depreciation schedule, investor's tax rate, initial purchase price, final sale price, and project holding period. This routine duplicates Section 1250 of the Internal Revenue Code. Capital gains profit is often the key factor in determining investor participation in a project.

Stage 13 calculates the yearly (monthly, if desired) interest and amortization payments and the year-end balance, given the initial mortgage, interest rate, and term. Interest payments are tax deductible while amortization payments build up the investor's equity position. The subroutine assumes a level payment mortgage and acts as a surrogate for a bond repayment table.

Stage 14 uses the information developed above to calculate profit in several forms: after-tax return on equity,[1] cash flow return on equity,[2] after-tax income plus capital gains profit return on equity,[3] and cash flow plus capital gains profit return on equity.[4] Before-tax income, after-tax income, yearly cash flow, and average equity are also calculated. Profitability is a time function and can be computed on a yearly basis or in the sale year. If the former holds, capital gains profit is omitted.

Stage 15 considers money's time value by discounting all future cash flows to the present, using the investor's discount rate, so they can be evaluated equivalently at a point in time. This is based on the view that one dollar received ten years from now is not equal to a dollar received one year from now. Investors prefer to receive as many dollars as possible early in a project's life for reinvestment in other profit-generating enterprises. The varying depreciation, interest, amortization, capital gains profit, operating expense, and rent flows require systematic analysis and evaluation. The present value and internal rate of return concepts fulfill this requirement.

HAM IN USE

HAM has shown its usefulness in, and has in turn been further improved and developed by, the New Jersey Housing Finance Agency. Specific public housing projects have been analyzed for cost and feasibility, and the State's housing program is being rethought with its aid. Ultimately it may guide New Jersey's legislative policy development.

The HAM program is on file in the Harvard Com-

---

[1] $$\text{After-tax return on equity} = \frac{\text{Average after-tax income}}{\text{Equity investment}}$$

[2] $$\text{Cash flow return on equity} = \frac{\text{After-tax cash flow}}{\text{Equity investment}}$$

[3] $$\text{After-tax} + \text{capital gains return} = \frac{\text{After-tax income} + \text{capital gain profit}}{\text{Equity investment}}$$

[4] $$\text{Cash flow} + \text{capital gains return} = \frac{\text{Cash flow} + \text{capital gain profit}}{\text{Equity investment}}$$

puter Center under a code name. Hook-up with the Harvard computer is through a teletype terminal in the Housing Finance Agency's Trenton office. This, plus long distance phone lines, connects the Trenton office with the Harvard Computer Center in Cambridge, allowing agency officials to use the model at will for daily decision making.

It is difficult in a short chapter to do justice to a subject as complex as the financial and economic aspects of residential real estate. HAM's power and sophistication are only hinted at in the flow diagrams given here. A number of subroutines are available for analyzing the following kinds of complex issues:

- What is the optimum holding period for a given housing investment, assuming a depreciation method, depreciable life, equity position, mortgage schedule, anticipated rents and operating expenses, and projected selling price?
- What is the trade-off between obtaining a long-term low-interest-rate mortgage on the basis of project longevity and minimizing the depreciable life of the project for tax purposes? The arguments involved are mutually contradictory.
- What is the relationship between the increased cost of higher quality and more durable construction and the better tax shield generated by a longer-term mortgage?
- What is the relationship between the additional investment required for operating-cost-savings materials or equipment and subsequent operating expenses over the project life?

Additional subroutines for analysis of special situations can easily be developed and plugged into the program. HAM is a practical and versatile tool for which a busy future can be anticipated.

Chapter Three

ANALYSIS AND INTERPRETATION

A systematic application of HAM to HUDA 68 involves a long series of computer operations. We have organized this series into a sequence of seventeen steps. These steps can be better understood when considered in three sections: Base Cases (BCs), Section 236 Program, and Other Programs. This chapter presents the analysis and interpretation of these steps. The detailed procedure and results of each step are presented in the Appendix.

Base Cases

The four BCs are the starting points of our analysis. They serve as bench marks against which changes in variables, assumptions, and estimates can be compared. They represent hypothetical projects, but every effort was made to describe "typical" conditions. Ideally, BC projects should be established for each geographical area, since project types, material costs, labor rates, taxes, and operating expenses vary from place to place. This range of BCs would yield a more accurate analysis of project costs and subsidy programs than the following generalized analysis. The localized BCs would also allow a more specific study of supply and demand requirements for the low-income housing market. Lack of data and time, however, prevented such detailed examination in this report. Certainly all low-income housing should conform to minimum health and safety standards, add attractively to its environment, and avoid the dangers of early obsolescence or tenant stigmatization. The BCs established are adequate in these respects as well as meeting all government specifications and cost limits. But this analysis has concentrated on quantitative rather than qualitative aspects of new or rehabilitated housing.

The BCs for new construction (BC1 and 2) and rehabilitation (BC3 and 4), respectively, are presented in Steps 1 and 3 of the detailed procedural outline which is found in the Appendix. Step 1 also performs a profitability analysis for the BC2 project. The BCs are tested for sensitivity to changes in selected cost categories in Steps 2 and 4, with the results summarized and interpreted in the following paragraphs.

BC Projects

Table I presents rental requirements and income levels served for the four BC projects. Each contains 100 new or rehabilitated housing units with a 1:3:3:1 ratio of one, two, three, and four-bedroom units. Average monthly rents range from $227 for BC1 to $170 for BC4. Equivalent income levels for these rentals, assuming 25% of the family income spent for rent, are $10,900 to $8,200, respectively. These are not low-income by any standard, and some form of subsidy will clearly be necessary. The applicability and effectiveness of subsidy programs will be considered later, but it will be useful first to examine the reasons for the BC's high rents and incomes. Understanding the projects' cost structures will allow more reasoned analysis of adjustments necessary to accommodate lower-income families.

Table I. Market Rents and Income Levels for Alternative Base Cases

Base Case Type	*Average Market Rents (per month)*	*Minimum Income Levels (per year)*
New construction, nonprofit (BC1)	$227	$10,896
New construction, limited-dividend (BC2)	224	10,751
Rehabilitation, nonprofit (BC3)	173	8,304
Rehabilitation, limited-dividend (BC4)	170	8,180

Table II summarizes input and output characteristics per BC unit developed in Exhibits 1 and 2 (pages 42 to 49 in the Appendix). Total development costs for new construction are approximately 45% higher than for rehabilitation.

Occupancy expenses, and thus rents and incomes, are approximately 30% higher for new construction projects. These differentials originate in the difference between land acquisition plus construction costs for new construction and land and building acquisition plus rehabilitation cost for the rehabilitation case. The difference ($17,404 per unit versus $12,000 per unit) is translated into the appropriate development fees, carrying and financing charges, and total development costs. The mortgage amount and equity position, debt service and profit requirements, and annual expenses are in turn calculated, establishing total occupancy expenses. The summary table traces interaction of these cost categories for the four BCs. Based on this cost structure, the rentals required and income levels served are determined, so it is essential to recognize the inherent relationships.

TABLE II. PER UNIT COST CATEGORIES FOR ALTERNATIVE BASE CASES

	Base Case Type			
	New Construction		*Rehabilitation*	
Cost Category	*Nonprofit* BC1	*Limited-Dividend* BC2	*Nonprofit* BC3	*Limited-Dividend* BC4
Land or land and building acquisition costs	$ 1,000	$ 1,000	$ 2,000	$ 2,000
Construction or rehabilitation costs	16,404	16,404	10,000	10,000
Development fees	2,493	3,385	1,657	2,240
Carrying and financing charges	2,259	1,714	1,625	1,295
Total development cost	$22,156	$22,503	$15,282	$15,535
Mortgage amount	$22,156	$20,253	$15,282	$13,982
Equity position	—	$ 2,250	—	$ 1,553
Annual debt service and profit requirements	$ 1,724	$ 1,712	$ 1,190	$ 1,181
Annual expenses	996	976	877	864
Total occupancy expenses	$ 2,720	$ 2,688	$ 2,067	$ 2,045
Total rent per unit per month	$ 227	$ 224	$ 173	$ 170
Minimum family income	$10,896	$10,751	$ 8,304	$ 8,180

The choice of new construction or rehabilitation has implications in addition to the effect on rents and income. Construction type should also be considered in relation to other factors associated with the housing project or the housing industry in general. Such factors include a consideration of the minimum property standards and economic life of the building, development term and scheduling, relocation, type of materials and labor, investor's profitability, and local participation or preferences. These considerations will be discussed as appropriate elsewhere, especially in relation to the federal expenditure required to achieve housing goals under alternative approaches. However, it is difficult to generalize on the pros and cons of new construction versus rehabilitation. Such analysis is best accomplished in terms of particular projects and local circumstances.

The alternatives of nonprofit versus limited-dividend sponsorship can be more easily generalized. The slight rent reduction for the limited-dividend sponsored projects is due to the following cost structure adjustments:

- The builder's profit for the nonprofit BC is replaced by a builder's and sponsor's profit and risk allowance for the limited-dividend BC; this allowance is double the normal builder's fee, consistent with the increased responsibility of the limited-dividend sponsor.
- The working capital provisions and housing consultant's fee are eliminated as separate items since it is assumed the sponsor will absorb these costs; part of the architect's fee is also paid out of the sponsor's allowance.
- Given the changes in assumptions above, total development costs are adjusted which in turn establishes a new basis for determining mortgage amount or equity position.
- The limited-dividend BC requires an equity investment equal to 10% of total development cost; the sponsor is allowed a 6% return per annum on this investment; for the nonprofit BC, 100% of total development cost is mortgaged and is subject to the market debt service factor; this factor is greater than the 6% limited-dividend distribution.

The limited-dividend alternative seems to have several advantages. Not only are rents and incomes reduced, but a portion of development costs is covered by equity capital, allowing available mortgage funds to be extended over more projects. Private equity investment also stabilizes the housing industry's historical counter-cyclical movement. The fact of the sponsor's real investment in the project also tends to increase personal responsibility during the development and occupancy periods. Such professional involvement is important for lower-income project success, especially in a project's early years. Nonprofit sponsored projects sometimes have failed for lack of proper organization and management. But these advantages can become disadvantages if the limited-dividend sponsor operates only to maximize his own profit position in developing and administering the project. The slight savings in rental requirements also may be lost if the effective debt service factor is reduced below the limited-dividend distribution. For these reasons, each project should be monitored and evaluated in its own terms.

Profitability Analysis

The 6% return on equity allowed the limited-dividend sponsor is an artificial standard. In itself it would not be sufficient to attract private equity capital for low-income housing investment. The limited-dividend sponsor in fact anticipates considerable tax benefits which when added to the 6% distribution will result in a sizable total cash flow. The sponsor also expects to realize a large capital gains profit from the project's future sale. A thorough profitability analysis is thus an essential part of the limited-dividend BC calculations. Such an analysis, performed for the BC2 project in Step 1 of the detailed procedural outline, is summarized in the following paragraphs.

This report concentrates on the evaluation of housing investments from the sponsor's viewpoint, recognizing that there are as many profitability measures as investors. The following analysis does not specify one criterion as better than another, but rather presents alternative criteria which can be applied and compared by the individual investor. Our methodology requires a five-stage sequence:

(1) Annual interest and amortization charges are calculated, assuming a yearly level annuity basis for mortgage repayment; the year-end mortgage balance and average equity, both original and accrued, are also determined.
(2) Yearly depreciation deductions are computed for tax purposes as well as the undepreciated balance; any of the four conventional depreciation methods can be employed, with an automatic shift from accelerated depreciation to the straight-line method when appropriate.
(3) The project's tax position and cash flows are determined for each year of the holding period using the first two stages' results; before-tax and after-tax incomes are calculated as well as total cash flow, subdivided into tax savings or taxes paid and limited-dividend distributions.
(4) Capital gains inflow is determined, assuming the project was sold at the end of each year; capital gains profit is defined as the selling price less the capital gains tax and the outstanding mortgage balance at the time of sale; the tax calculations duplicate Sections 1231 and 1250 and the Cohn Rule of the Internal Revenue Code.
(5) Three measures of equity return in each year are calculated using the previous stages' results: average after-tax, average cash flow, and average cash flow and capital gains inflow; net present values of the project are also determined during each year of the holding period and as if there were a sale at the end of each year; these are the alternative profitability criteria that could be used by investors in evaluating housing investments.

Graph 3 summarizes the implications of interest and amortization and depreciation calculations, the limited-dividend distribution and annual expenses for a 25-year period. Shaded areas in the graph equal the difference between project revenues and the tax position after all deductions have been made which, in effect, represents before-tax income. In the project's early years, total allowable deductions (interest + depreciation + annual expenses) are greater than revenues so that a potential tax shelter results. Assuming the investor can apply this tax shelter against other taxable income, there is a tax savings which is added to the cash flows. As tax deductions decrease over time, this shelter is reduced; after the 23rd year, a taxable income results. The taxes to be paid after this point would be reflected in the cash flows.

Since annual project expenses are more or less constant relative to revenues, interest and depreciation deductions are the primary determinants of taxes. For a level annuity repayment schedule of the 6.75%, 40-year mortgage assumed in this analysis, interest payments comprise most of the debt service requirements in the early years, gradually declining until amortization payments become dominant. Amortization, representing an accrued equity, is not deductible and must be accounted for in the cash flows. Investors interested primarily in their tax position rather than equity position naturally prefer the interest payments to remain dominant for as long as possible. Fortunately, because of the nature of the level annuity repayment schedule, the point of equilibrium between interest and amortization does not occur until the later years. Interest deductions can also be restored at an appropriate time through refinancing, but this option has not been evaluated here.

Depreciation deductions are less automatic functions requiring more critical investor decisions involving the choice of depreciable life and depreciation methods. Depreciable life is tied to economic life and mortgage term but with some flexibility. Depreciating a project over a short life concentrates tax deductions in the early years; a long life spreads deductions over more years. Similarly, the four standard depreciation methods distribute tax deductions in different proportions over a longer or shorter period. This analysis assumed a 200% double-declining balance depreciation method over a 25-year life, converting in the 14th year to the straight-line method, a shift that is allowed once under existing tax rules. This depreciation schedule combined with interest deductions creates a large tax shelter early in the holding period, which, however, deteriorates rapidly as allowable depreciation decreases. An investor anticipating a sale in the early years would want to maximize the tax benefits in this way, if he could apply the resulting tax savings against some other form of income. If he wished to hold the project for a longer period, or had no way to use the tax savings, he would select an increased depreciable life or choose a less accelerated depreciation method. For example, it can be shown that had the straight-line method been used from the onset for a 25-year life, the tax shelter would be equalized and extended, such that no taxes would be paid during this term. It should be noted that the accumulated difference between accelerated and straight-line depreciation is determined for the first

Graph 3. Tax Position vs. Years of Holding: New Construction, Limited-Dividend (BC2)

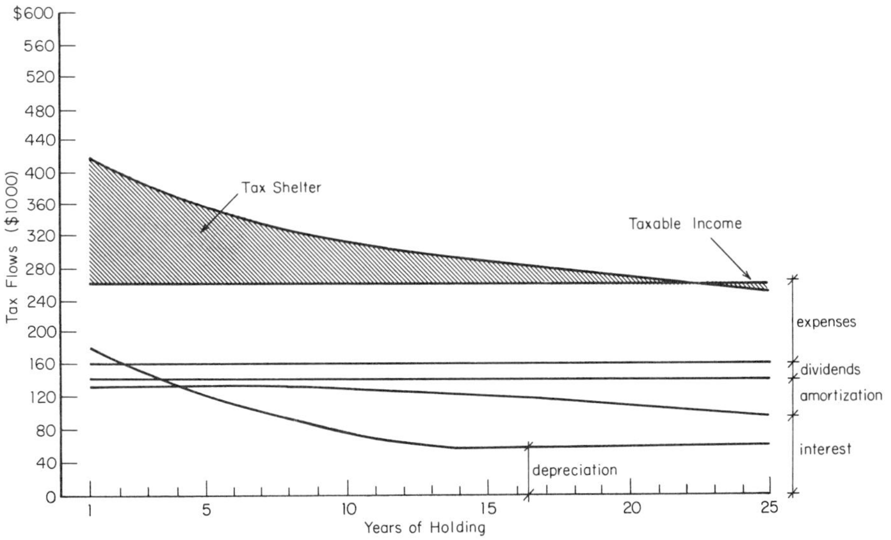

ten years of project life for use in capital gains tax calculations. Excess depreciation would, in effect, be recaptured by a sale in the early years, reducing net benefits of the tax shelter created. This illustrates the point that profitability factors are interrelated and should not be treated in isolation.

Graph 4 presents project profit flows over a 25-year period. These flows are total cash flow, capital gains profit, and the combined flow and profit. Original equity and average equity are also plotted for reference purposes. It seems from this graph that the capital gains profit is the critical factor. Up to year 10, capital gains profit and total cash flow are in relative balance, but thereafter profit is dominant. It should be recognized that capital gains profit is really a hypothetical flow, since the project could not be sold in each year. But the capital gains profit does determine total profitability and is often the basis for the decision to invest in a project and the length of time to hold it. On the other hand, total cash flow represents an annual return which can be taken out each year. In fact, accumulated cash flow + capital gains profit should be evaluated together by the investor to determine the optimum holding period.

GRAPH 4. PROFIT POSITION VS. YEAR OF HOLDING OR SALE: NEW CONSTRUCTION, LIMITED-DIVIDEND (BC2)

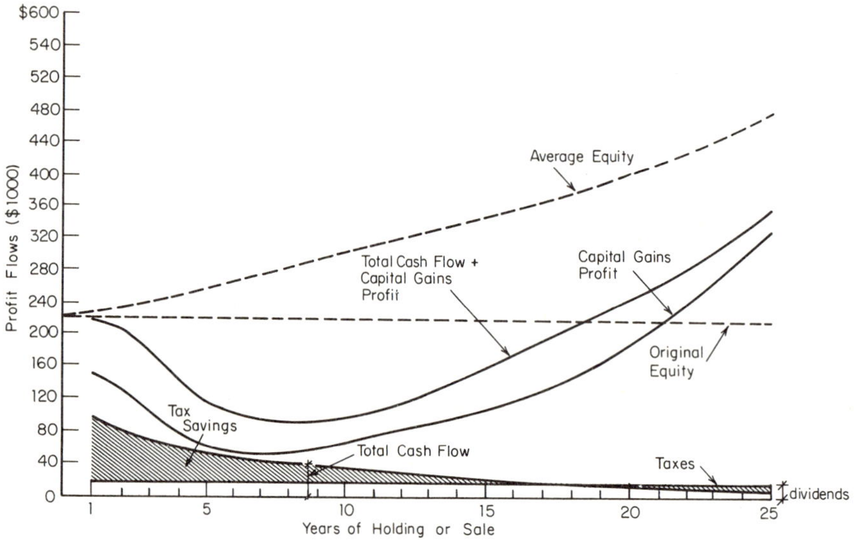

The total cash flow in a given year is subdivided into the limited-dividend distribution plus any tax savings, or less taxes paid. Total cash flow can also be represented by the following profit and loss statement:

Total Project Revenue
less: Annual Expenses
Interest Charges
Depreciation Deductions
Real Estate Taxes

Taxable Operating Income
less: Taxes Paid or plus: Taxes Saved

After-Tax-Income
Total Cash Flow = Taxes Paid or Saved + 6% Limited-Dividend Distribution

Tax savings or taxes paid equal the tax rate times before-tax income plotted in the previous graph. Negative before-tax income represents a loss, but we assume that the investor has other taxable income available so that losses are actually translated into a tax savings; that is, the investor does not have to pay taxes which would normally be incurred if the project's tax shelter was not available. Total cash flow declines over the first 23 years as tax deductions are reduced. In years 24 and 25, taxes must be paid, reducing the total cash flow below the fixed limited-dividend distribution level. As mentioned earlier the point at which taxes are paid could be postponed by selecting an alternative depreciable life or depreciation method, extending the mortgage, or refinancing. Any of these adjustments would also reduce the total cash flow during this period, however. Again, the compromise is between greater average short-term profits or smaller average long-term profits.

The investor can also sell the project when annual returns decline, reinvesting in a more attractive project.

Capital gains profit resulting from a sale goes through three phases, the graph's changing slope being a function of the following parameters in any given year: depreciable life, depreciation method, mortgage interest rate and amortization term, tax provisions for treatment of capital gains, and depreciation recapture rules. For a holding period less than 20 months, all gains are taxed at the investor's ordinary income rate. For periods greater than 20 months but less then 10 years, part of the gain is taxed at ordinary rates and part at the long-term capital gains rate which is half the ordinary rate. The proportion of recognized capital gains taxed at ordinary versus capital gains rate is determined by the number of months from point of sale to year 10. During this period the accumulated difference between the accelerated and straight-line depreciation enters the calculations. After 10 years all gains are taxed at the long-term capital gains tax rate, so the slope evens out once again.

The capital gains position is a function of several factors; if any factor is changed, subsequent adjustments are made which may affect the holding period. For example, reducing depreciable life to 15 years to increase the early years' tax shelter also increases capital gains tax as a result of the additional depreciation. The investor will want to seek a longer holding period to avoid heavy recapture. Note that for this analysis recognized capital gain was calculated assuming a selling price equal to the purchase price. Many investors speculate that property values are going to appreciate rapidly. If correct, the investor makes a substantial capital gain profit which completely overshadows annual cash flows. This dominance of capital gains position over cash flow position is often the reason for the short holding period of many projects.

Graph 5 presents profitability criteria developed from previous results; Graph 6 plots net present project values during the normal holding period and assuming a sale at the end of a given year. Profitability criteria help determine a moving average of a project's performance in generating a return on equity. They act as a control or warning device to monitor or adjust profit flows. For example, average after-tax return relates the flow available in terms of tax shelter. In year 12, this return has decreased to 19.39%. If the investor's assumed opportunity cost tied to this criterion was 20%, he would re-evaluate his current investment. If tax considerations were primary, and alternative investments were available at a higher return, he would be wise to sell this project and reinvest in one yielding a greater average after-tax return. Similarly, the average cash flow criterion allows investment evaluation predicated on cash flow return. Either criterion can be used as an indicator, which, when compared with indexes of capital cost, anticipated return, opportunity cost, or some other cut-off criterion, would point to positive or negative profit performance and ultimately trigger the decision to sell.

Average cash flow + capital gains inflow return is often the critical criterion for project profitability decisions, due to the dominance of capital gains profit, given a year-end sale, compared to normal after-tax and cash flow returns. In a project's early years, this capital gains inflow imbalance is particularly pronounced, but it averages out as after-tax or cash flow returns accumulate. Again, this accounts for the frequent short holding periods for housing investments. If holding-period returns motivated the investor to re-evaluate his position in the project, he would then determine his rate of return assuming sale. The result will establish whether he should sell or delay further, according to his cut-off criteria. The two stage decision process is outlined below:

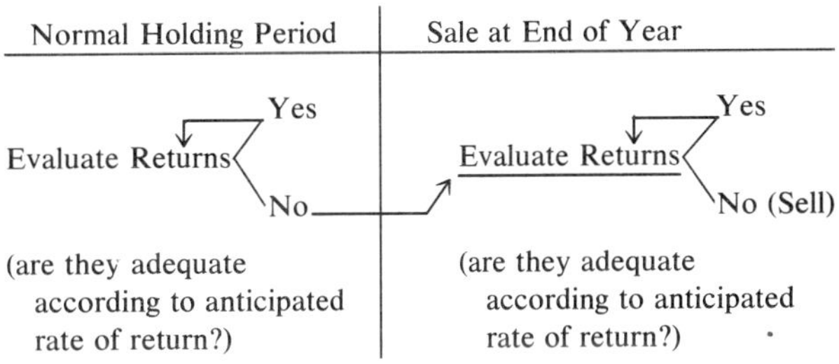
Normal Holding Period
Sale at End of Year
Yes
Evaluate Returns
No
(are they adequate according to anticipated rate of return?)
Yes
Evaluate Returns
No (Sell)
(are they adequate according to anticipated rate of return?)

Net present values during the holding period, or in case of sale, are calculated by discounting all project inflows and outflows back to year 0 and summing the results. The investor's discount rate has been selected as 15% in these calculations. Net present value, assuming the project is held, never reaches a maximum within the 25-year period plotted but does reach a point of diminishing returns by year 15.

This type of profitability analysis can also evaluate tax incentive programs designed to stimulate private investment. For example, a new program might provide for shorter depreciable life, investment tax credits, relaxed capital gains tax or recapture provisions, or other incentives. Each provision and combination of provisions can be tested for impact on the investor's tax position, rate of return, probable

GRAPH 5. PROFITABILITY CRITERIA VS. YEAR OF HOLDING OR SALE: NEW CONSTRUCTION, LIMITED-DIVIDEND (BC2)

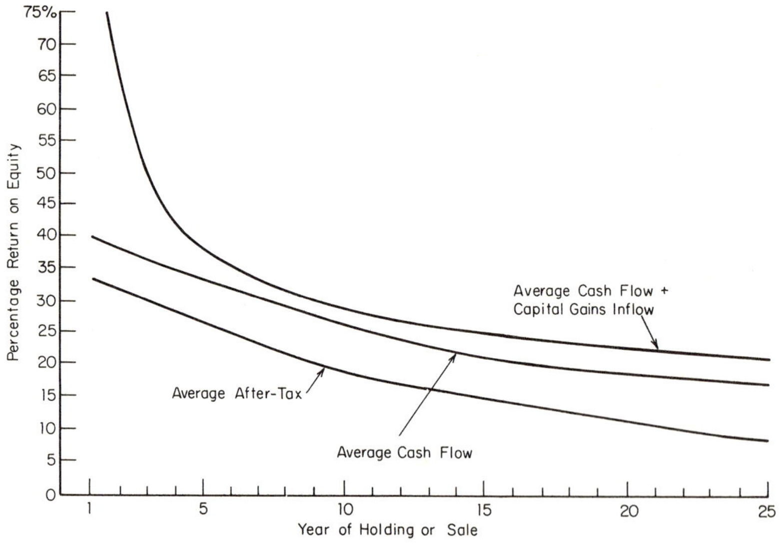

GRAPH 6. PRESENT VALUE VS. YEAR OF HOLDING OR SALE: NEW CONSTRUCTION, LIMITED-DIVIDEND (BC2)

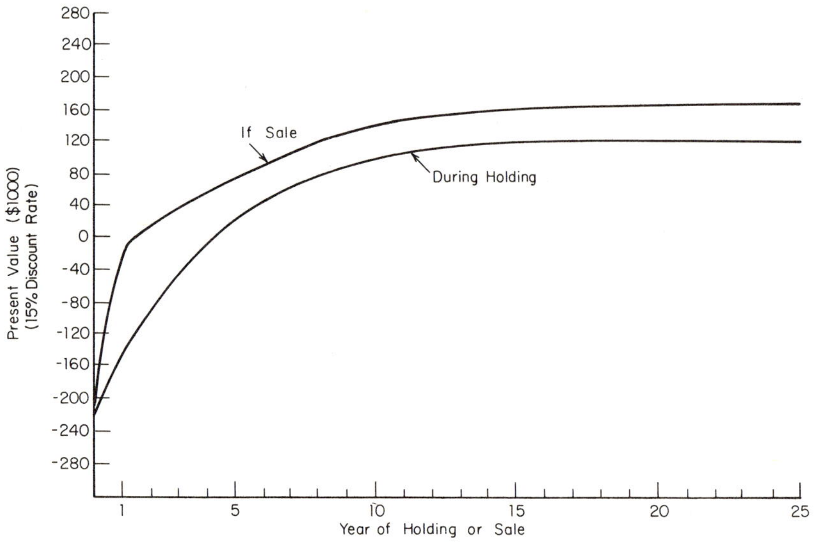

holding period, and so forth. Trade-offs could be defined and an optimum program developed to satisfy the required objectives. Similarly, this profitability analysis could be applied to other government housing programs to evaluate incentives or disincentives for private investment. This report has not attempted the analysis in terms of HUDA 68's provisions, which would require considerable additional study.

BC Variations

The nonprofit BCs are tested under a series of changes in major cost categories: land acquisition cost, construction or rehabilitation cost, interest rate, mortgage term, operating expenses, and real estate taxes. (The percentage of income spent for rent is also tested but does not actually comprise a cost category as it only affects the proportion of a family's budget spent for housing.) This testing demonstrates the cost structure's sensitivity to such variations as measured by rentals and income levels. For example, a 30% construction cost increase with all other variables held constant results in an average BC rent increase from $227 to $258 per month and in average income levels from $10,900 to $12,400 per year. It is important to understand the cost structure relationships and the impact of cost changes on this structure to evaluate subsidy programs later in this report. Table III and Graphs 7 and 8 present selected cost changes, summarizing Steps 2 and 4 of the detailed procedural outline.

The first relationship relevant to a specific cost variable's impact is the number of additional cost structure factors it affects. This measure provides an approximation only since several small changes may not be as effective as one or two major changes. Such multiple changes may be desirable for other reasons, however, such as equalizing costs for mortgage purposes, reducing the property tax base, and so forth. In any event, tracing these changes provides a useful cost structure review. This example compares subsequent effects of an initial construction cost change versus operating expenses:

Initial Change: Construction Cost ↓

Subsequent Changes:
- Development Fees
- Financing and Carrying Charges
- (Total Development Cost)
- (Mortgage Amount)
- Debt Service and Profit Requirements
- Real Estate Taxes
- Contingencies
- (Total Occupancy Expenses)
- (Rentals and Income Levels)

Initial Change: Operating Expense ↓
- Real Estate Taxes
- Contingencies
- (Total Occupancy Expenses)
- (Rentals and Income Levels)

The cost categories may be ranked according to subsequent changes in other cost components as shown at the top of the next column.

A cost variation's impact is also partly a function of the particular variable's dominance in the cost structure. For example, land costs comprise 1/22 or 4.5% of total development costs for new construction, while construction costs comprise 16/22 or 72.8%. Respective ratios for the same cost categories for rehabilitation are 2/15 or 13.3% and 10/15 or

Cost Category	*Number of Cost Components Influenced*
Construction or rehabilitation costs	9
Land and building acquisition	8
Debt service as a function of rate	4
Debt service as a function of term	4
Operating expenses	4
Real estate taxes	3

66.7%. A given percentage change in a more dominant cost category will produce a greater effect on rents and incomes than a corresponding change in a lesser category. This is shown in the tables and graphs where a 30% construction cost decrease reduces rents from $227 to $180 (21%), but a 30% land cost decrease reduces rents only to $225 (1%). However, a 30% rehabilitation cost decrease reduces rents from $173 to $144 (17%) while a similar reduction in land and building acquisition costs reduces rents to $168 per month (3%). The differences in a given percentage cost change's effect on the two BCs could have been predicted from the ratios established. The acquisition cost/total development cost ratio for new construction was less than the same rehabilitation ratio by a factor of about three, which is also the rent change factor. The differentials that exist between this approximation and calculated rents result from the effect of certain independent cost variables which are not affected by land acquisition cost changes. For example, operating expenses do not change if land or any other development cost is varied, so these changes are not passed through

TABLE III. EFFECT ON MARKET RENTS AND INCOME LEVELS OF SELECTED COST VARIATIONS: NEW CONSTRUCTION AND REHABILITATION, NONPROFIT (BC1 AND BC3)

Base Case Variations		*Average Market Rents (per month)*		*Minimum Income Levels (per year)*	
		BC1	BC3	BC1	BC3
Market base case		$227	$173	$10,896	$ 8,304
Land acquisition cost	−50%	223	164	10,688	7,887
	+50%	231	181	11,091	8,694
Construction cost	−30%	180	144	8,660	6,918
	+30%	273	201	13,105	9,654
Interest rate at	4.75%	188	146	9,025	7,001
	8.75%	269	202	12,932	9,702
Mortgage term of	50 years	221	168	10,601	8,090
	30 years	240	182	11,511	8,720
Operating expenses	−30%	212	157	10,155	7,555
	+30%	242	188	11,624	9,025
Real estate taxes (Gross shelter rent method)		224	170	10,752	8,160
Income factor of	15%	227	173	18,149	13,817
	35%	227	173	7,773	5,921

proportionately. These fixed variables create distortions if such ratios are applied indiscriminately for large changes.

The relative effects of different cost variations are represented in the graphs. The slopes define a multiplier for each cost category:

$$\text{Multiplier} = \frac{\text{Change in Rents}}{\text{Change in Cost Category}}$$

The larger the multiplier, the greater a cost variation's impact on the cost structure. Cost categories are ranked according to decreasing multiplier effects below:

New Construction

1. Construction costs
2. Interest rate
3. Mortgage term
4. Operating expenses
5. Land acquisition cost

Rehabilitation

1. Rehabilitation costs
2. Interest rate
3. Operating expenses
4. Mortgage term
5. Land and building acquisition cost

Rankings for alternative BCs are the same except for items 3 and 4, because of cost structure proportions. For new construction, debt service requirements comprise 63.4% of total occupancy expenses versus 36.6% for the annual expenses. For rehabilitation, respective percentages are 57.6% and 42.4%. Thus, a 10% reduction in operating expenses affects a lesser percentage of total occupancy expenses under new construction than under rehabilitation, resulting in a lesser change in rents. The opposite relationship exists for variations in the mortgage term but with an additional complication. Mortgage term is an exponential function of the debt service factor according to the formula:

$$\text{debt service factor} = \frac{i}{1 - \dfrac{1}{(1+i)^n}}$$

where i = interest rate percentage
n = mortgage term in years

In other words, changing mortgage term 10% does not change the debt service factor by 10%, while changing operating expenses 10% reflects directly in the cost structure. These difficulties in trying to compare percentage changes relative to some common base led to the development of absolute comparisons. These are explained below.

Table IV shows the relative effectiveness of $100,000 subsidies applied to each of the six major cost categories. These measures provide a common denominator for assessing the impact on rents and

GRAPH 7. CHANGES IN AVERAGE RENT VS. CHANGES IN SELECTED COST VARIABLES: NEW CONSTRUCTION, NONPROFIT (BC1)

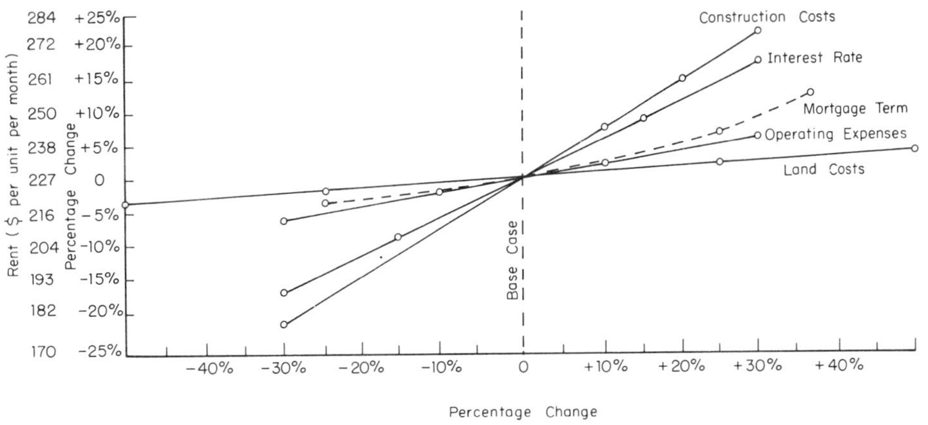

GRAPH 8. CHANGES IN AVERAGE RENT VS. CHANGES IN SELECTED COST VARIABLES: REHABILITATION, NONPROFIT (BC3)

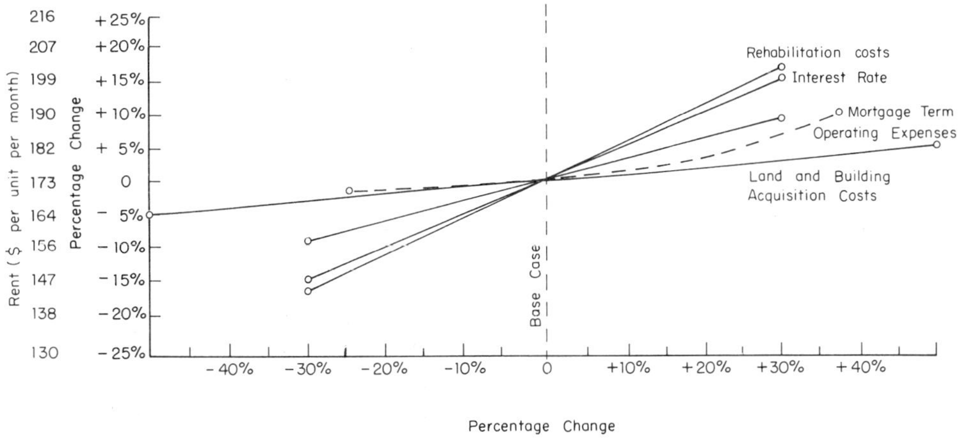

incomes, and they eliminate the problems encountered in comparing percentage variations. For development period changes in land or construction costs, the subsidy amount is characterized by a lump sum payment in year 0, as either direct transfers to the developer or indirect transfers within government housing agencies which would eventually be translated into a development cost or mortgage reduction. Occupancy period changes take the form of 40 year-end payments (except for the mortgage term case as noted). The yearly reduction in interest charges, amortization charges, operating expenses, or real estate taxes is found by dividing the $100,000 annuity compounded at a 5% interest rate by the present value of the total number of year-end payments. The lump sum or annualized payments, percentage reduction in the cost category, and absolute and percentage reductions in rents are recorded in the tables for comparison.

The change ranking indicates the most efficient way to allocate the $100,000 subsidy for rent reduction per dollar spent. The order of effectiveness was the same for both new construction and rehabilitation, given our assumptions, but other BCs with more dissimilar cost structures may exhibit differences in the subsidy impact and should be tested separately. The following ranking, therefore, should not be generalized:

1. Construction or rehabilitation cost
2. Land and building acquisition
3. Debt service payment as a function of interest rate
4. Debt service payment as a function of mortgage term

TABLE IV. RELATIVE EFFECTIVENESS OF ALTERNATIVE $100,000 SUBSIDIES: NEW CONSTRUCTION AND REHABILITATION, NONPROFIT (BC1 AND BC3)

Cost Category	*Type of Subsidy*	*Amount of Subsidy**	*Percentage Change in Cost Category*		*Absolute Reduction in Average Rents*	*Percentage Reduction in Average Rents*	
			BC1	BC3		BC1	BC3
Land costs	Lump sum payment in year 0	$100,000	−100%	−50%	$ 9/month	4%	5%
Construction costs	Lump sum payment in year 0	100,000	−6	−10	10/month	4.5	6
Debt service payment as function of interest rate	Annualized payment for 40 years	5,828/yr.	−4	− 5	6/month	3	4
Debt service payment as function of mortgage term	Annualized payment for 49 years (BC1)** for 56 years (BC3)	5,504/yr. 5,348/yr.	−3.5	− 4.5	6/month	3	4
Operating expenses	Annualized payment for 40 years	5,828/yr.	−12	−12	6/month	3	4
Real estate tax	Annualized payment for 40 years	5,828/yr.	−23	−21	5/month	2	3

*The yearly reductions in interest charges, operating expenses, and real estate taxes are found by dividing $100,000 in toto by the present value of 40 payments compounded annually at a 5% rate of interest. The $100,000 represents the present value of an ordinary annuity of 40 year-end payments.

** The reduction in debt service charges resulting from an increase in the mortgage term is computed by dividing $100,000 by the present value of 49 year-end payments compounded at a 5% rate of interest. The $100,000 represents the present value of an ordinary annuity of 49 year-end payments.

5. Operating expenses
6. Real estate taxes

Note that this ranking corresponds to the numerical order of subsequent cost components affected in the cost structure. Ranking the multipliers by percentage changes in a cost category was different in several respects.

In all three lists, however, the cost change which affected rents and incomes most was construction or rehabilitation cost, supporting those advocating research and development efforts aimed at controlling or reducing these costs. However, the most optimistic estimate of cost savings resulting from such efforts is approximately 10%. For our BC assumptions, a 10% reduction in this cost category would yield a rent reduction of only 8% and 5.5% for new construction and rehabilitation, respectively. How much time, energy, and resources, then, should be allocated to research and development for future savings versus direct subsidy payments in other cost categories to achieve rent reductions? In any event, costs must be controlled or reduced simultaneously in many categories, or a savings in one may be more than offset by an increase elsewhere.

It should also be recognized that annualized subsidy payments are in certain respects better value for money than lump-sum payments. Since the $100,000 amount is not spent all in one year but treated as an ordinary annuity, the expenditure is compounded. If the discount were to increase, the subsidy amount available for occupancy period cost reductions would also increase. At some point, these categories could become the most efficient type of subsidy. Other factors such as land value appreciation, construction materials and labor price increases, availability of mortgage funds or equity capital, market interest rate ceilings, operating cost inflation, and real estate tax changes also influence the relative effectiveness of alternative subsidies. Furthermore, the timing of government expenditures in terms of the national budget, the administrative costs of different subsidy programs, and similar considerations should be taken into account in assessing the desirability of lump-sum versus annualized subsidy payments. Such a cost/benefit analysis is beyond the scope of this report, but it is an essential subject for future attention.

Section 236 Program

Section 236 assists rental and cooperative housing for lower-income families, by way of periodic payments to the mortgagee on behalf of the mortgagor, to reduce rent. The payments make up the difference between the amount required for principal, interest, and mortgage insurance premium on a mortgage at the market interest rate and the amount required for principal and interest on a mortgage at a 1% rate. The Section 236 basic rents are calculated by adjusting the required market rent by the allowable periodic payment. The tenant is charged this basic rental or 25% of his monthly income, whichever is greater. However, the effective rental cannot exceed what the fair market rental would be if the project received no assistance. Receipts in excess of the basic rental are returned to the Federal Government. (See Diagram E.)

DIAGRAM E
Section 236 Subsidy Formula

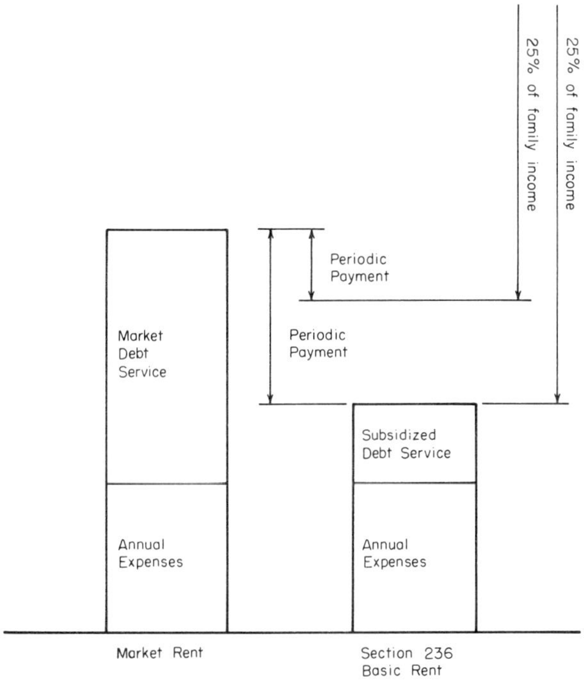

The Section 236 Program is designed to replace, when fully operative, the 221(d)3 Below Market Interest Rate (BMIR) Program which provided 3% financing of low- and moderate-income housing. In addition to reducing the interest rate from 3% to 1%, the Section 236 subsidies go directly to the mortgagee as periodic payments. Under 221(d)3 BMIR, the mortgagee made the initial below market interest rate loan, but it was immediately purchased by the government through the Federal National Mortgage Association (FNMA), paying the lender a handling charge. The mortgage could subsequently be discounted, making up the difference between the 3% rate and the market rate, and resold. Or FNMA could service the mortgage for the entire term. This procedure required large expenditures at each point of transfer for either purchasing or discounting the mortgage.

Since these secondary mortgage market operations had to be funded out of general government revenues in a given year, necessitating an increase in the national debt ceiling, the 221(d)3 BMIR Program's effectiveness was severely limited by immediately available resources. Under the Section 236 Program, private financing is secured initially and permanently, and the government does not need to handle the mortgage at all. Furthermore, subsidy commitments are spread over the mortgage term through the periodic payments. This approach should give the government better leverage, for a given expenditure, in providing lower-income housing.

The economic analysis of the Section 236 Program is detailed in Steps 5 through 12 of the procedural outline in the Appendix. In Steps 5 through 10 basic rents and minimum and maximum income levels are calculated by application of the subsidy formula to the four BC projects and combinations of these projects. The number of new or rehabilitated housing units possible with various annual appropriations for the program is also determined. In Steps 11 and 12, the effects of changes in BC1 and BC3 are tested, calculating and comparing their impact on rents, incomes, and number of units provided. The following paragraphs summarize and interpret these results.

Average market and basic rents and basic income levels for the alternative BCs are shown in Table V. This table and similar tables for other portions of this report contain two additional indexes referred to in the analysis. The periodic payment for each BC type is shown. It equals the difference between subsidized and unsubsidized rents as calculated under the subsidy formula. This payment represents the absolute amount of rent reduction and is also used as the basis for determining how many housing units are possible with a given annual appropriation. A percentage index is entered as well, relating the percentage reduction from unsubsidized to subsidized rents; this is useful for ranking the subsidies' impact on the alternative BC types.

TABLE V. SECTION 236 RENTS AND INCOME LEVELS FOR ALTERNATIVE BASE CASES

Base Case Type	*Average Market Rents (per month)*	*Average Section 236 Basic Rents (per month)*	*Minimum Section 236 Income Levels (per year)*	*Periodic Payment (per month)*	*Percentage of Subsidization*
New construction, nonprofit (BC1)	$227	$140	$6,718	$87	38.2%
Rehabilitation, nonprofit (BC3)	173	113	5,403	60	34.6
Mixed * nonprofit	195	124	5,952	71	36.4
New construction, limited-dividend (BC2)	224	144	6,912	80	35.6
Rehabilitation, limited-dividend (BC4)	170	115	5,520	55	32.5
New construction, mixed ** (BC1 and BC2)	225	142	6,816	83	34.9
Rehabilitation, mixed ** (BC3 and BC4)	171	114	5,472	57	33.3

* One-half of the appropriation is used to subsidize new construction projects and one-half for rehabilitation. The numbers presented in this column are the weighted average rents and income levels for new and rehabilitated units provided under the allocations. The weighting scheme used is 40% of new units and 60% of rehabilitated units.

** One-half of the appropriation is used to subsidize nonprofit sponsored projects and one-half for limited-dividend. The numbers presented in these columns are the weighted average rents and income levels for nonprofit and limited-dividend sponsored units in new construction and rehabilitation projects respectively. The weighting scheme used is 48% nonprofit sponsored units and 52% limited-dividend.

Section 236

The Section 236 Program can reduce rents and provide housing for families in lower-income sectors that otherwise could not afford new or rehabilitated housing. For BC1, the average market rents of $227, subsidized through a periodic payment equivalent to $87 per month, result in an average basic rent of $140, representing a 38.2% reduction. The respective minimum income levels required to support such rents, assuming 25% of family income spent for rent, similarly decline by 38.2% from $10,900 to $6,700 per year. Average rents and income levels for the other BC projects and mixed projects are also reduced by approximately 35%.

Additional interpretations can be drawn from this table, summarizing Steps 5 through 10 of the procedural outline. Rehabilitation projects produce the lowest absolute rents and incomes, both subsidized and unsubsidized, because of lower original development costs and subsequently lower occupancy expenses. However, the percent reduction of rents, applying the subsidy formula, is greater for new construction than for rehabilitation projects. This is because higher development costs for new construction result in higher debt service requirements. The project can therefore absorb more interest rate subsidies, although never to the extent of equalizing the absolute rents.

Another apparent relationship is that nonprofit sponsored projects produce lower rents and incomes under Section 236 subsidies than limited-dividend sponsored projects for the respective BC types. This is particularly striking since the limited-dividend alternative generally produced lower rents and incomes under market conditions. The reason for this reversal is that nonprofit sponsored projects have higher debt service requirements based originally on a mortgage which is 100% of project value, but the total mortgage amount is eligible for the interest rate subsidies. Only 90% of a limited-dividend project value is mortgaged, reducing the debt service requirements that can be subsidized.

Conclusions about the Program's effectiveness based on rent and incomes alone should be deferred, however, until the next aspect of the analysis is surveyed. Table VI and Graphs 9 and 10 summarize the units possible with various annual appropriations for the different BC types. The projections are calculated by dividing the allowable periodic payment under the subsidy formula into the assumed appropriation. It takes approximately $1,000 each year to subsidize a new construction unit and $700 for a rehabilitated unit. Put another way, for each $1,000 of subsidy, one new construction unit or one and one-half rehabilitated units can be provided. These are approximations only, and the differences among

TABLE VI. EFFECT OF SECTION 236 APPROPRIATIONS ON THE NUMBER OF UNITS PROVIDED, APPLIED TO ALTERNATIVE BASE CASES

	Number of Units Provided						
	Nonprofit			*Limited-Dividend*		*Mixed*	
Annual Appropriations	*New* BC1	*Rehab.* BC3	*Mixed**	*New* BC2	*Rehab.* BC4	*New* †	*Rehab.* †
$10,000,000	9,589	13,857	11,723	10,500	15,210	10,025	14,500
25,000,000	23,973	34,642	29,307	26,250	38,000	25,100	36,300
50,000,000	47,946	69,285	58,615	52,500	76,000	50,250	72,650
75,000,000	71,918	103,927	87,922	78,750	114,000	75,350	108,950

* One-half of the appropriation is used to subsidize new construction projects and one-half for rehabilitation. The numbers presented in this column are the total of new and rehabilitated units provided under the allocations. On the average, the total is composed of 40% new units and 60% rehabilitated units.

† One-half of the appropriation is used to subsidize nonprofit sponsored projects and one-half for limited-dividend. The numbers presented in these columns are the total number of nonprofit and limited-dividend sponsored units in new construction and rehabilitation projects, respectively, provided under the allocations. On the average, the total is composed of 48% nonprofit sponsored units and 52% limited-dividend.

GRAPH 9. ANNUAL SECTION 236 APPROPRIATIONS VS. NUMBER OF UNITS PROVIDED: ALTERNATIVE SPONSORSHIP *

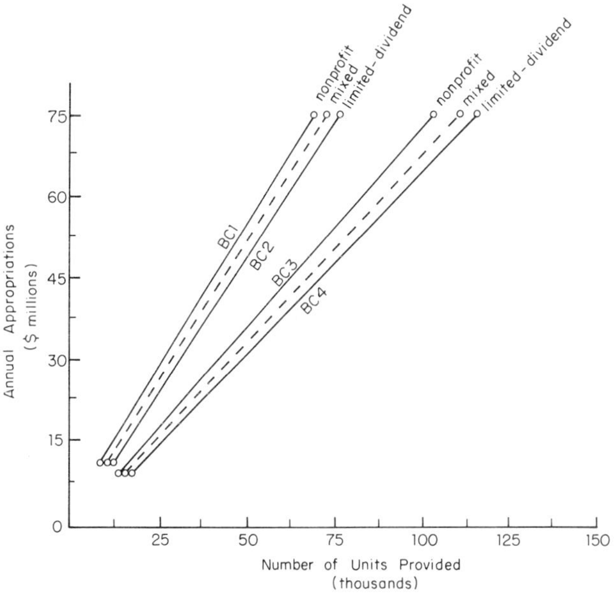

* The same level of appropriation is used to subsidize new construction under nonprofit, limited-dividend, and mixed sponsorship.

GRAPH 10. ANNUAL SECTION 236 APPROPRIATIONS VS. NUMBER OF UNITS PROVIDED: NEW CONSTRUCTION AND REHABILITATION,* NONPROFIT (BC1 AND BC3)

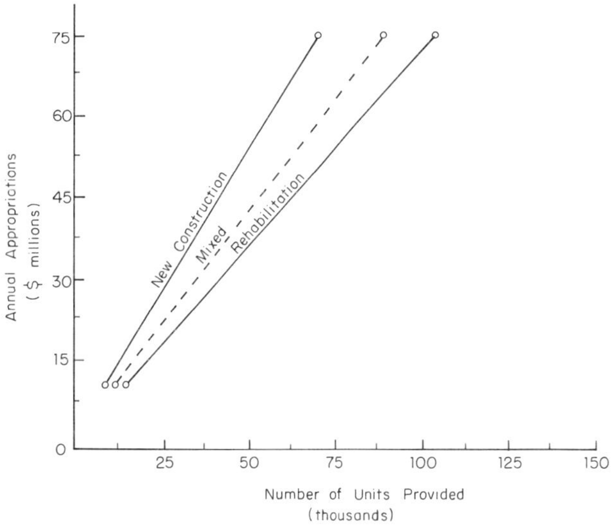

* The same level of appropriation is used under nonprofit sponsorship to subsidize new construction, rehabilitation, and mixed projects.

BC types are important for understanding the Program's impact.

More rehabilitated units can be provided than new construction units under a given appropriation because of the lower rehabilitation development costs. The mortgage amount and debt service requirements based on these development costs are also lower, and a smaller periodic payment is required per average unit under the Section 236 formula. Thus a given appropriation can assist more units. The relationship between nonprofit and limited-dividend sponsored projects is less obvious. The differential in the number of units provided for a BC results from the limited-dividend projects having only 90% of their value mortgaged, resulting in a smaller allowable periodic payment per average unit. Interest rate subsidies can be spread over more units. By comparing the new construction columns for nonprofit and limited-dividend, this factor of .90 can be clearly seen. The slight discrepancy is due to the difference in original development cost for the two projects.

Combining the implications of the above conclusions, there appears to be a dilemma. On the basis of rents and incomes, nonprofit sponsorship offers lower absolute rents and higher percentage subsidization, whereas limited-dividend sponsorship provides more units. The question becomes whether to provide fewer units at lower rental charges and incomes served or more units with higher rents and incomes. A combined strategy will in fact spread the appropriations over a wider range of the lower income sector. This policy dilemma can be more easily resolved given the projections contained here, though the choice and justification of a particular policy alternative lie outside this report's scope.

A similar dilemma exists between the alternatives of new construction and rehabilitation. The rehabilitation BC projects produce the lowest absolute rents and incomes and provide the most units for a given appropriation, but new construction projects can be subsidized to a greater extent. The question becomes, considering standards, specifications, and economic life of new versus rehabilitated units, whether to provide more rehabilitated units at lower rents and incomes, or fewer new units with higher standards and longer life at higher rents and incomes. Again, a mix of approaches is probably desirable, combining the advantages of increased standards and life for new units with the decreased costs and subsidies for rehabilitated units. The graphs for BC and sponsorship combinations clearly define the compromises.

Section 236 Three-Year Projections

With Tables V and VI it is also possible to project the units possible under the cumulative appropriation levels authorized (but not yet funded) for the Section 236 Program. These authorizations are:

$ 75	million through fiscal 1969
+100	million through fiscal 1970
+125	million through fiscal 1971
$ 300	total authorization

Thus by the end of fiscal 1971, $300 million could be available annually for Section 236 assistance. (Only $25 million was actually appropriated for fiscal 1969, with $50 million additional on stand-by approval.) If all units were of the BC1 type, a maximum average periodic payment per unit of $1,044 each year would be allowable, and 285,876 new units could be subsidized annually with a $300 million appropriation. Average subsidized rent would be $140 per month and the equivalent family income level, $6,718 per year. For the BC3 type, maximum average periodic payment per unit would be $720 each year, or 415,710 rehabilitated units subsidized annually at average rents of $113 per month and a $5,403 income level. If a BC1 and BC3 mix were the average condition, a periodic payment of $852 each year would be required and 351,690 units could be provided; the average of average rents would be $124 per month and the income level, $5,952.

The Department of Housing and Urban Development reportedly anticipates that 500,000 units could be subsidized under the Section 236 Program with a $300 million annual appropriation. Working backwards, this represents an average periodic payment per unit of $600 per year. Under the Section 236 subsidy formula, assuming a 6.75%, 40-year mortgage and a maximum interest rate reduction to 1%, this payment translates into an average subsidized rent of $100 per month and a $4,800 income level. The $150 market rent is based on a $1,200,000 total development cost for 100 new or rehabilitated housing units in a nonprofit sponsored project.

There are several possible reasons for the apparent discrepancies between this report's projections and the government projections. Most obvious is the low development cost, $12,000 per average unit, implicit in the government calculations. Our BC costs, based on typical projects from field experience, are probably more realistic. As shown on the facing page, BC3 corresponds to the maximum legislated mortgage limits and BC1 corresponds to the exception limits for high cost areas. Historically,

Number of Bedrooms	*Legislated Limits* *Mortgage Amount*	*Mortgage Amount* + 45%	*Base Cases* BC1	BC3
1	$11,250	$16,400	$15,500	$10,700
2	13,500	19,600	19,900	13,800
3	17,000	24,600	24,400	16,800
4	19,250	27,900	28,800	19,900
average unit	$15,200	$22,000	$22,150	$15,300

projects have been built to the maximum limits and, if anything, these limits should be revised upwards in urban areas.

Note that our projections are based on multiples of 100-unit projects. There is thus a linear relationship between number of units provided and assumed annual appropriation, with no returns to scale as expenditures increase. With higher appropriations, larger projects would probably be built, resulting in cost savings, or other economies would result from the increased volume of housing starts; such savings would then reduce the periodic payments required per unit and stretch available subsidies over more units. For instance, with a volume of about 50,000 units a year, an industrialized building system may be feasible. The authorized appropriations of $300 million could easily account for this volume, and real cost savings could result from application of industrialized methods. Government projections may anticipate such factors.

We also assumed that each unit receives the maximum allowable annual subsidy. In practice no unit, or at least not the average, may receive the maximum periodic payment, resulting in appropriations being allocated to more units, but increasing required rents and income levels accordingly. For example, if average BC1 periodic payments were reduced from $87 to $60 per month, the units possible with the $300 million annual appropriation would increase from 285,876 to 415,710, but average rentals would increase from $140 to $167 per month and equivalent incomes would increase from $6,718 to $8,016. The government projections may have assumed some percentage of the maximum allowable periodic payment as its average condition, effectively spreading the available subsidies over a wider income range. It is questionable whether this distribution can assist a significant number of truly low-income families.

This distribution, even if not determined initially, is likely to occur by itself over time. We assumed that the maximum allowable periodic payment per unit would be applied over the entire mortgage period. However, family incomes will probably increase gradually over time, decreasing the required subsidy. The subsidy formula explicitly anticipates such increases in income, stating that the allowable periodic payment shall be the lesser of the difference between market rate debt service requirements and a 1% rate requirement, or 25% of family income. This further enables a family gradually to improve its income without jeopardizing its right to assisted accommodation. When 25% of family income equals the market rent, periodic payments effectively reduce to zero. However, a family will not be required to move because of an increase in income. This should help stabilize family and community situations and remove some of the "project" stigma.

The government is gaining good leverage with this approach since it assists housing at current cost levels with commitments which can be expected to decrease over time. It is not clear, however, what will happen to excess periodic payments returned to the government, whether they will be used to reduce annual appropriations in later years or applied to additional projects. Assuming the latter, further adjustments can be made in our projections. Incomes should increase by a rough average of 3% per year. The table on page 28 indicates the additional BC1 units at the maximum subsidy possible with application of excess periodic payments to other units as incomes increase. The Section 236 basic rent in year one is determined on the basis of the allowable interest rate reduction and in subsequent years as 25% of family income as inflated. The required periodic payment equals the difference between market and basic rent in each case. For the maximum periodic payment, 285,876 units can be provided. Reduced periodic payments in later years for this number of units divided into the total annual appropriation of $300 million equals the surplus subsidy available, which is then apportioned to determine the additional units provided at the maximum periodic payment.

Year	*Market Rents*	*Income Level*	*Section 236 Basic Rents*	*Periodic Payment*	*Number of Additional Units*
1	$227	$ 6,718	$140	$87	–
5	227	7,785	162	65	74,510
10	227	9,065	189	36	169,120
15	227	10,490	218	9	258,090
16	227	10,800	226	1	282,630

In this illustration a complete cycle would take place in just over 16 years, but it is a great oversimplification to consider income increases in isolation. Annual housing expenses (other than debt service requirements which are fixed) would also probably increase at a rate of 3% or more. Furthermore, development costs per housing unit probably will be much higher in later years, requiring a greater average periodic payment and making fewer units possible with a given appropriation. A net inflation factor relating incomes and costs should be applied to predict and control the Program's impact over the term of its operation.

Selected Cost Variations

Steps 11 and 12 of the procedural outline test effects of changes in cost variables, assumptions, and estimates for BC1 and BC3 respectively. Tables VII and VIII summarize and compare these selected cost changes' effects in the BCs. The effects are measured in terms of market rents, basic rents and incomes, and the new or rehabilitated units provided under various appropriations. Results from a given variation are predictable in general: a 30% cost increase for new construction results in an increase in rents and incomes and a decrease in the number of units provided, and vice versa. This variable testing gives insights into not only general sensitivities of the BC cost structure, but also specific sensitivities of the Section 236 subsidy formula.

These variations' general relationships have been detailed for the BCs under market conditions. The more interesting issue for the Section 236 Program pertains to differentials of change between unsubsidized rents and incomes and differentials in the units provided. To get a fix on these differentials, certain indexes have been entered in the tables for reference in the analysis. The first index represents the percentage reduction from market rents under BC conditions to subsidized rents and incomes for a cost variation. A useful relationship that these indexes can determine is the percentage change in subsidized rents and incomes under the cost variations. This is accomplished by subtracting the index for subsidized rents and incomes from the index for BC market rents. For the 30% construction cost decrease, the change is (35.6 − 38.2 =) −2.6%; a construction cost increase results in a change of (40.4 − 38.2 =) +2.2%. Comparison of these changes indicates the relative effect of a similar increase or decrease in a variable. It is apparent that the Section 236 subsidy formula is less sensitive here to a construction cost increase than to a decrease. Different variables' effects can also be compared using this index.

The other entries in these tables refer to periodic payments applicable under the subsidy formula for each variation. The number of units provided is calculated by dividing this periodic payment into the assumed appropriation. The ratio of the periodic payment for the BC under market conditions to the payment for a cost variation indicates the percentage change in units provided. For example, for the new construction BC with a 30% construction cost decrease, the ratio is 87/64 which represents an increase in the units provided of 35.9%. The tables include this factor. These indexes relating rents, incomes, and the units provided will be referred to frequently below in the analysis of cost change effects on the Section 236 Program. (For brevity, only the new construction BC changes will be detailed except where a special relationship exists for rehabilitation.)

Construction cost variations increase or decrease the development cost, which in turn affects mortgage amount. The subsidy formula reduces debt service requirements based on this mortgage amount, but cost changes can only be absorbed proportionately. This is shown in the percentage reduction for an increase in construction costs, which is 40.4% versus 38.2% for the BC, a small differential in subsidy, considering the increase or decrease in absolute costs. Rents also increase, from $140 to $163 per month, for this variation, primarily because of the higher debt service requirements calculated for the

TABLE VII. EFFECT OF SELECTED COST VARIATIONS ON SECTION 236 RENTS AND INCOME LEVELS:
NEW CONSTRUCTION AND REHABILITATION, NONPROFIT (BC1 AND BC3)

Base Case Variations		Average Market Rents (per month) BC1	BC3	Average Sec. 236 Basic Rents (per month) BC1	BC3	Minimum Income Levels (per year) BC1	BC3	Periodic Payment (per month) BC1	BC3	Subsidization BC1	BC3
Section 236 Base Case		$227	$173	$140	$113	$6,718	$5,403	$87	$60	38.2%	34.6%
Construction Costs	−30%	180	144	116	98	5,590	4,709	64	46	35.6	31.9
	+30%	273	201	163	127	7,839	6,093	110	74	40.4	36.8
Bedroom Mix #1		165	129	101	83	4,858	4,979	64	46	38.9	35.7
Bedroom Mix #2		291	220	180	144	8,633	6,917	111	76	38.1	34.6
Interest Rate at	5.75%	207	159	135	109	6,497	5,251	72	50	34.8	31.4
	7.75%	248	187	143	115	6,882	5,517	105	72	43.3	38.5
Operating Expenses	−30%	212	157	125	97	5,983	4,669	87	60	41.0	38.3
	+30%	242	188	155	128	7,453	6,138	87	60	35.9	31.9
Income Factor of	15%	227	173	140	113	11,197	9,006	87	60	38.2	34.6
	35%	227	173	140	113	4,799	3,860	87	60	38.2	34.6

TABLE VIII. EFFECT OF SECTION 236 APPROPRIATIONS ON NUMBER OF UNITS PROVIDED
WITH SELECTED COST VARIATIONS:
NEW CONSTRUCTION AND REHABILITATION, NONPROFIT (BC1 AND BC3)

Number of Units Provided

Annual Appropriations	Sec. 236 BC	Construction or Rehabilitation Costs −30%	+30%	Bedroom Mix #1	Bedroom Mix #2	Interest Rate at: 5.75%	7.75%	Operating Expenses −30%	+30%
BC1:									
$10,000,000	9,589	13,020	7,595	12,950	7,520	11,650	7,945	9,589	9,589
25,000,000	23,973	32,590	18,988	32,400	18,790	29,110	19,850	23,973	23,973
50,000,000	47,946	65,180	37,975	64,800	37,580	58,230	39,700	47,946	47,946
75,000,000	71,918	97,770	56,962	97,200	56,780	87,340	59,550	71,918	71,918
Percentage change in units provided	—	+35.9%	−21.0%	+35.9%	−21.6%	+21.0%	−17.1%	0.0%	0.0%
BC3:									
$10,000,000	13,857	18,110	11,233	17,970	10,990	16,830	11,584	13,857	13,857
25,000,000	34,642	45,270	28,082	44,930	27,440	42,070	28,960	34,642	34,642
50,000,000	69,285	90,540	56,165	89,850	58,870	84,130	57,920	69,285	69,285
75,000,000	103,927	135,810	84,248	134,780	82,310	126,200	86,840	103,927	103,927
Percentage change in units provided	—	+30.2%	−18.9%	+30.2%	−21.1%	+19.9%	−16.7%	0.0%	0.0%

1% rate on the new mortgage amount. However, rents are also affected by increases in operating expenses, taxes, and contingencies which are indirectly based on development costs.

A change in mortgage amount also influences the units that can be provided. A decrease reduces the periodic payment required for debt service subsidy, and conversely. For new construction, a 30% increase in construction costs increases the required payment from $87 to $110 per month and the number of new units that can be provided under a given appropriation thus decreases by a factor of 87/110 or 21.0%. For a 30% decrease in construction costs, the ratio is 87/64, or a 35.9% increase in the units provided. This differential is consistent with the fact that proportionately less subsidy can be absorbed under the construction cost increase than the decrease. The net effect is that with a cost increase rents cannot be subsidized to the desirable extent, but, on the other hand, the reduction in the number of units provided is smaller.

Interest rate variations are more critical. The maximum allowable subsidy is determined by the difference between the effective market rate debt service factor and 1% rate factor. Clearly, a reduction in the effective rate will decrease the subsidy required and vice versa. For the new construction BC, a 5.75% rate results in a rent reduction of 34.8% and a 7.75% rate in a 42.3% reduction. The increases or decreases seem absorbed by the subsidy formula until the absolute rents and incomes are compared. For the 5.75% rate, rents have been reduced from $140 to $135 per month, but for the 7.75% rate rents have increased from $140 to $143 per month. It would seem on first reading the Section 236 Program that rents should have been equal in each instance. The differences are due to the subsidy formula used to calculate basic rents. On the basis of these rents, the other annual expenses are calculated. Certain of these expenses, such as real estate taxes and contingencies, are taken as a percentage of total project income, which includes the market rate debt service requirements. Periodic payments under the subsidy formula then reduce market rents, but the results have already been affected by the increases or decreases in annual expenses. This procedure can be defended in part. It would be unfair, for example, to undercut the local tax base by calculating taxes in terms of the 1% mortgage rate. A reasonable alternative would be to assess some negotiated tax payment in lieu of taxes in proportion to reduced rents. On the other hand, there can be no argument for the mortgagor to determine contingencies on the total debt service requirements, since all but 1% of this amount will be guaranteed by federal periodic payments. Since calculations for this analysis were completed, HUD has issued guidelines indicating that the allowable vacancy and collection losses will be adjusted in some fashion for Section 236 projects to balance the subsidy formula. HUDA 68 also states that market and basic rent calculations will be subject to approval by federal authorities. Perhaps these discrepancies will be eliminated in practice, but as the subsidy formula now stands the selection of market interest rate will indirectly affect rents and incomes.

Interest rate variations have a more pronounced effect on units provided. Again, the amount of the periodic payment equals the difference between the effective market rate debt service factor and a 1% rate factor. Reducing the interest rate to 5.75% correspondingly reduces the periodic payment and increases units that can be provided. A ratio of 87/72, or a 21.0% increase, represents this difference in required periodic payments. Increasing the interest rate to 7.75% decreases the units possible by 87/105, or 17.1% (The differential is due to the nonlinearity of the debt service factor; that is, the level annuity debt service factor is calculated as an exponential function of interest rate and amortization term.) Thus, variations in interest rate apparently have relatively little effect on project rents and incomes, since the subsidy formula directly compensates for the changes. However, since interest rate differentials are absorbed, the units provided increase or decrease proportionately. Fiscal and monetary policy makers should be aware of these considerations and their impact on achieving the nation's stated housing goals.

Variations in operating expenses demonstrate further limitations of the Section 236 subsidy formula. Decreasing operating expenses for the new construction BC results in a 41.0% rent and income reduction. Absolute value of the rents decreases from $140 to $125 per month. For an increase in operating expenses, an increase of 35.9% results, with an absolute increase from $140 to $155 per month. This relationship is opposite that of other cost changes; that is, the percentage reduction under the subsidy formula is greater for cost decreases than for cost increases, because periodic payments under the variation equal the BC payment. In other words, the changes affect operating expenses independently of the subsidy formula. Decreasing expenses will decrease rents, because of both direct and indirect reductions, in terms of other annual expenses calculated as a percentage of total project income. However, since the periodic payment remains constant, the units provided are not affected. Similarly, increasing operating expenses increases rents and incomes but does not change the units provided. That no reduction occurs in the number of units is an advantage, but it is a disadvantage that the subsidy formula does not absorb the operating expense increases. This will be an important limitation in the Section 236 Program, especially in high cost urban areas where operating expenses are often a very significant factor in total rents. The subsidy formula will not offer relief under such circumstances, underscoring the need for careful project design and management to minimize the impact of operating expenses.

Unit distribution variations combine the effects of changes in construction costs and changes in operating expenses according to the assumptions given for alternative bedroom mixes. As has been discussed, a change in construction or rehabilitation costs results in a change in development costs with a corresponding change in mortgage amount. Debt service requirements based on this mortgage amount are thereby affected, as are other annual expenses calculated as a percentage of total project income, and this changes the rents and incomes. The variation in mortgage amount is also reflected in the required periodic subsidy payment, which in turn affects the units that can be provided. Operating expense variations result in changes in rents and incomes, but these increases or decreases are independent of debt service requirements. Therefore, periodic payments under the subsidy formula are not affected and the units provided remain unchanged.

For BC1, this combined impact of construction cost and operating expense variations is demonstrated. For bedroom mix #1 with more small units, the reduction is 39.9%, decreasing absolute basic rents from $140 to $101 per month for the BC. For bedroom mix #2, with more large units, the reduction is 38.1%, with a change in absolute basic rents from $140 to $180 per month. The subsidy formula only partially affects cost increases or decreases, as was predicted. This could prove to be a limitation of the program, since lower-income families often require larger accommodations. For number of units provided, bedroom mix #1 has a periodic payment ratio of 87/64 resulting in a 35.9% increase. Bedroom mix #2 has a ratio of 87/111, a decrease of 21.6% in the number of units. These results are consistent with the fact that the units provided are affected by construction costs through the mortgage amount but not affected by operating expenses. Comparing the columns for construction cost changes taken independently, this relationship is apparent. In summary, the rents and incomes are affected by a combination of construction cost and operating expense variations assumed for the bedroom mixes, but the numbers of units provided are affected by construction costs only.

Variations in the percentage of family income spent for rent has no effect on either subsidized rents and incomes or the units provided. These rent/income ratios are used only to establish the standard proportion of a family's budget that should be allocated to housing. A lower percentage is considered desirable by many who recognize the other demands on a low-income family's budget, but such a standard would clearly make many low-income families ineligible for the rents projected under the Section 236 Program. For new construction, the $140 basic rent would translate into a required income of $11,197 per year at a 15% income factor for rent. A higher factor choice would have the opposite effect of bringing more low-income families into the eligibility range, but this artificial relaxing of standards probably would place a disproportionate burden on the families served.

Summary

Variable testing indicates important relationships in the Section 236 subsidy formula. Rents and incomes under a given variation are a function of cost increases or decreases affecting the mortgage amount and the subsidy formula operating on debt service requirements based on this mortgage amount. Rents and incomes are also affected, independent of the subsidy formula, by changes in annual expenses, due both to direct and indirect changes calculated in terms of mortgage amount. The units provided are a function of the periodic payment only, but the periodic payment changes do not necessarily correspond to the changes in rents and incomes. These relationships can be summarized in terms of particular variations tested as follows:

- Construction or rehabilitation cost changes affect both rents and incomes and the units provided; however, the subsidy formula does not operate to absorb the full impact of the changes, so rent differentials result. To the extent that changes are absorbed, the number of units provided changes.
- Interest rate variations affect primarily the units provided; the subsidy formula absorbs almost all the differential in effective interest rate, but periodic payments are subsequently adjusted, resulting in changes in the number of units provided.
- Operating expense variations affect only rents and incomes; the subsidy formula does not compensate for changes in operating expenses, so there is no possible effect on the units provided.
- Unit distribution variations combine the effects of changes in construction costs and changes in operating expenses: both affect rents and incomes and the units provided; the subsidy formula absorbs construction cost changes but does not compensate for operating expense changes.
- Variations in the percentage of income spent for rent have no effect on either rents or the units provided: this factor operates outside the subsidy formula to determine the income level required to support a given rent.

Other Subsidy Programs

HUDA 68 established or amended several subsidy programs to provide assistance to lower income families, in addition to the Section 236 Program. These programs are analyzed in detail in Steps 13 through 17 of the procedural outline and the results are summarized below:

- Section 235 provides assistance via periodic payments to the mortgagee for occupants to reduce effective housing costs, similarly to Section 236, except it is intended to assist home ownership rather than rental accommodation. The subsidy formula is also similar in part, calculating the maximum allowable periodic payment as the difference between the monthly payment for principal, interest, and mortgage insurance premium on a market rate mortgage, and the monthly payment for principal and interest due on a 1% mortgage. However, an additional test is that the periodic payment cannot exceed the balance of the monthly payment for principal, interest, insurance premium, real estate taxes, and home insurance under the market rate mortgage after applying 20% of the home owner's income. The latter limitation probably will be effective in practice for determining eligibility. (See Diagram F.)
- Section 221(h) provides assistance for rehabilitation of substandard or deteriorating structures for sale to lower income families. The program was amended by HUDA 68, reducing the below market interest rate from 3% to 1% and extending the appropriations. Section 221(h) and the other 221 BMIR programs are antecedents of the new Section 235 and 236 Programs, and will be phased out as the latter become operative. However, subsidy formulas differ under old and new programs. (See Diagram G.)
- Rent Supplements provide assistance through supplement payments directly to the mortgagor on behalf of lower income families. The appropriations for this program were extended by the 1968 Act. Payment amounts cannot exceed the difference between market rents and 25% of the tenant's income, but in any event are not to be less than 10% or more than 70% of market rents. The Rent Supplement Program is an effective and flexible method of adjusting rents for particular income requirements, especially when combined with other subsidy programs. (See Diagram H.)
- The Public Housing Program was significantly extended through increased appropriations by HUDA 68. Under the program, the entire debt service requirements are subsidized by annual federal contribution payments to the local housing authority. The project real estate taxes and contingency allowances are also reduced through the program. This total subsidy formula is capable of producing truly low-rent accommodations. (See Diagram I.)
- Section 506 is extended by HUDA 68 to cover land writedowns for open space land. Under this program's

DIAGRAM F
Section 235 Subsidy Formula

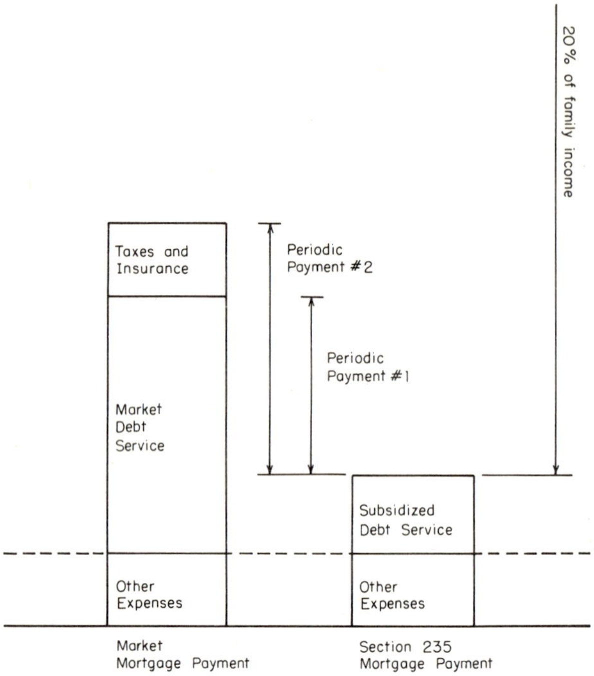

DIAGRAM G
Section 221(h) Subsidy Formula

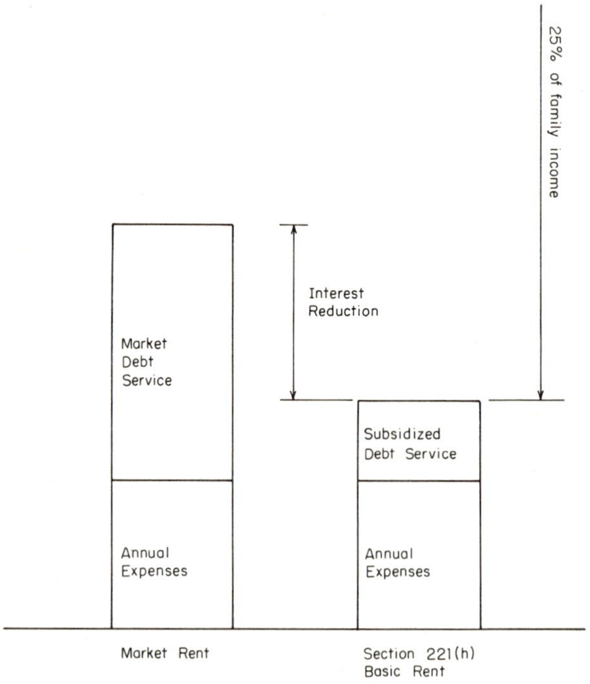

DIAGRAM H

RENT SUPPLEMENT SUBSIDY FORMULA

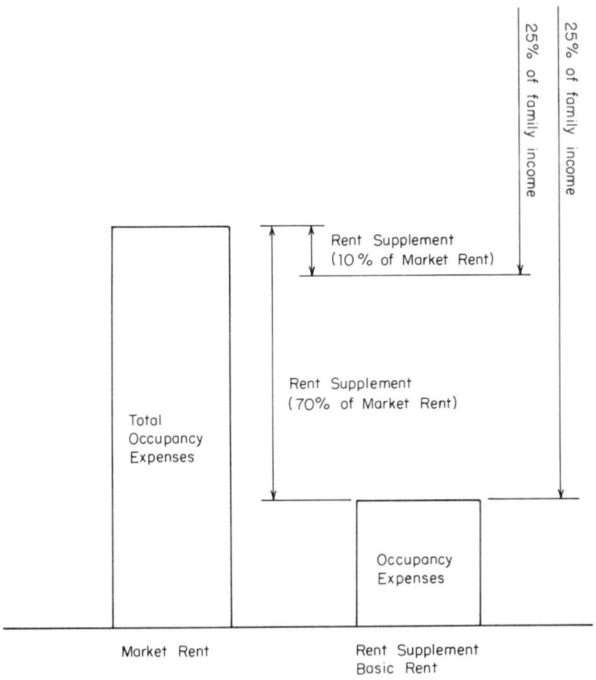

DIAGRAM I

PUBLIC HOUSING SUBSIDY FORMULA

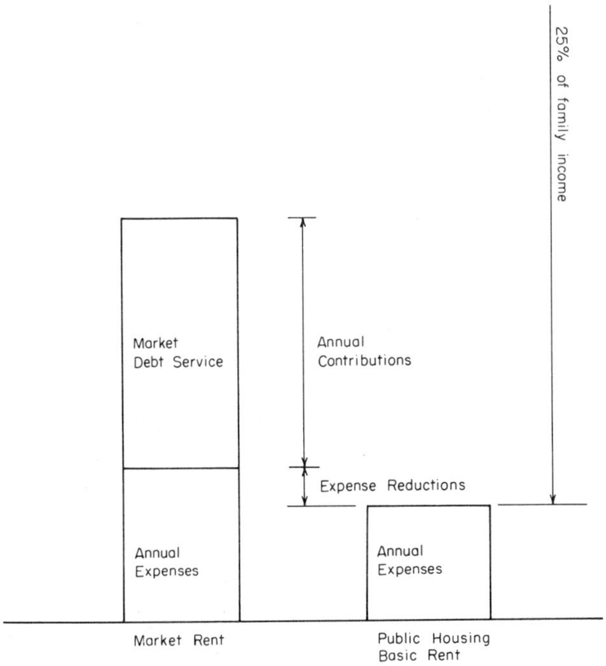

DIAGRAM J

SECTION 506 SUBSIDY FORMULA

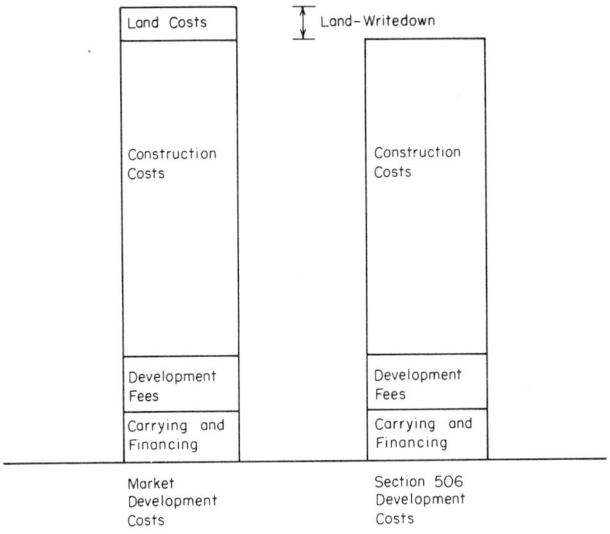

basic provisions, land can be acquired through outright purchase or eminent domain condemnation at market value, then transferred to an approved project developer at greatly reduced costs. This land writedown subsidy is particularly useful for low-income housing projects in urban areas where land values are high and would constitute a disproportionate amount of new or rehabilitated housing costs. (See Diagram J.)

Economic analysis of these "other subsidy" programs is detailed in steps 13 through 17 of the procedural outline. In each step, basic rents and minimum income levels are calculated under subsidy formulas for respective programs applied to new construction and rehabilitation (nonprofit) BCs. The units of new or rehabilitated housing possible with various annual appropriations for these programs are also determined. Results of this detailed analysis are summarized and interpreted in the following paragraphs. Each program's impact is determined independently, but suggestions are also made as to the effectiveness of applying combined subsidies.

Table IX presents average market and basic rents and basic income levels for alternative BCs. The units possible under various annual appropriations are shown in Table X and represented in Graphs 11 and 12. The tables also contain additional indexes which will be referred to in this analysis. A percentage factor is entered, relating the percentage reduction from subsidized to unsubsidized rents, an index useful in ranking the impact of subsidy programs. Each program's subsidy amount is also indicated,

TABLE IX. RENTS AND INCOME LEVELS FOR OTHER SUBSIDY PROGRAMS: NEW CONSTRUCTION AND REHABILITATION, NONPROFIT (BC1 AND BC3)

Subsidy Program Type	*Average Basic Rents (per month)*		*Minimum Income Levels (per year)*		*Subsidy Amount (per month)*		*Percentage Subsidization*	
	BC1	BC3	BC1	BC3	BC1	BC3	BC1	BC3
Market Base Case	$227	$173	$10,896	$8,304	—	—	—	—
Section 236	140	113	6,718	5,403	$ 87	$ 60	38.2%	34.6%
Section 235 *	57 (86)	40 (61)	3,390 (5,140)	2,420 (3,670)	65 (65)	47 (47)	53.4	54.1
Section 221(h)	N.A.	113	—	5,427	—	60	—	34.6
Rent Supplements	68	52	3,264	2,496	159	121	70.0	70.0
Public Housing **	75 (85)	69 (76)	3,615 (4,080)	3,290 (3,648)	152 (142)	104 (97)	66.9 (62.6)	60.2 (56.2)
Section 506 †	218	154	10,464	7,416	N.A.	N.A.	4.0	10.9

* Based on mortgage payments for BC1 dwelling cost of $17,500, which at market rates equals $122 per month; BC3 cost is $12,500, market rate is $87. The minimum income level is calculated as 20% gross family income spent for these payments. The numbers in parentheses represent 20% of gross family income spent for principal, interest, real estate taxes, and insurance.

** Based on subsidy of both debt service requirements and operating expenses. The numbers in parentheses represent the reduction due to debt service subsidy only, which is used as the basis for the projections of number of units provided.

† Based on a lump sum subsidy during development.

TABLE X. EFFECT OF APPROPRIATIONS ON THE NUMBER OF UNITS PROVIDED BY OTHER SUBSIDY PROGRAMS: NEW CONSTRUCTION AND REHABILITATION, NONPROFIT (BC1 AND BC3)

Annual Appropriations	*Number of Units Provided*											
	Section 236		*Section 235*		*Section 221(h)*		*Rent Supplements*		*Public Housing*		*Section 506*	
	BC1	BC3	BC1*	BC3†	BC1	BC3	BC1	BC3	BC1	BC3	BC1	BC3
$10,000,000	9,589	13,857	12,716	17,823	N.A.	13,857	5,257	6,896	—	—	10,000	5,000
25,000,000	23,973	34,642	31,790	44,620		34,642	13,142	17,223	—	—	25,000	12,500
50,000,000	47,946	69,285	63,580	89,240		69,285	26,285	34,446	30,980	44,925	50,000	25,000
75,000,000	71,918	103,927	95,370	133,860		—	39,427	51,669	—	—	—	—
100,000,000	—	—	—	—		—	—	—	61,960	89,850	—	—
Percentage Change in Units Provided	—	—	+33.9%	+22.6%	—	0.0%	−45.3%	−50.4%	−38.7%	−38.1%	+4.2%	−63.9%

* Based on dwelling cost of $17,500.

† Based on dwelling cost of $12,500.

representing the rent reduction's absolute value. This amount is used to determine the housing units possible with a given appropriation. The ratio of the Section 236 BC condition subsidy amount to amounts for other subsidy programs is entered in the projection tables, representing the change in units provided under alternative forms of subsidy. It should be noted, however, that the relationships between subsidy programs are not fully comparable at face value. Certain rents, subsidy amounts, and numbers of units provided are not based on the same BC assumptions and therefore must be qualified. These differences have been specified in footnotes to the tables and graphs and will be discussed as appropriate below.

These subsidy programs are clearly effective in reducing rents and providing for families that otherwise could not afford new or rehabilitated housing. For example, the $173 per month average market rents for the rehabilitation BC are reduced to $52 under the Rent Supplement Program, a subsidy of $121, or 70.0%. Respective minimum income levels required to support such rents are similarly reduced by 70.0%, from $8,300 to $2,500 per year. Assum-

GRAPH 11. ANNUAL APPROPRIATIONS FOR OTHER SUBSIDY PROGRAMS VS. NUMBER OF UNITS PROVIDED: NEW CONSTRUCTION, NONPROFIT (BC1)

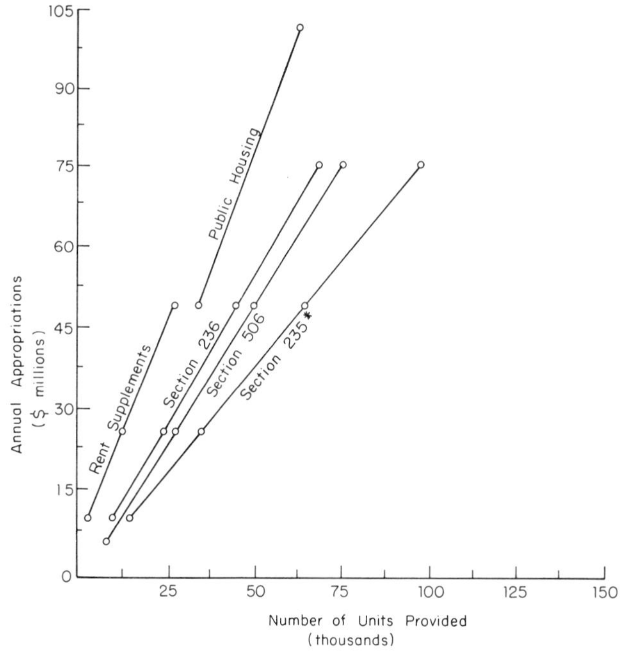

* Based on dwelling cost of $17,500.

GRAPH 12. ANNUAL APPROPRIATIONS FOR OTHER SUBSIDY PROGRAMS VS. NUMBER OF UNITS PROVIDED: REHABILITATION, NONPROFIT (BC3)

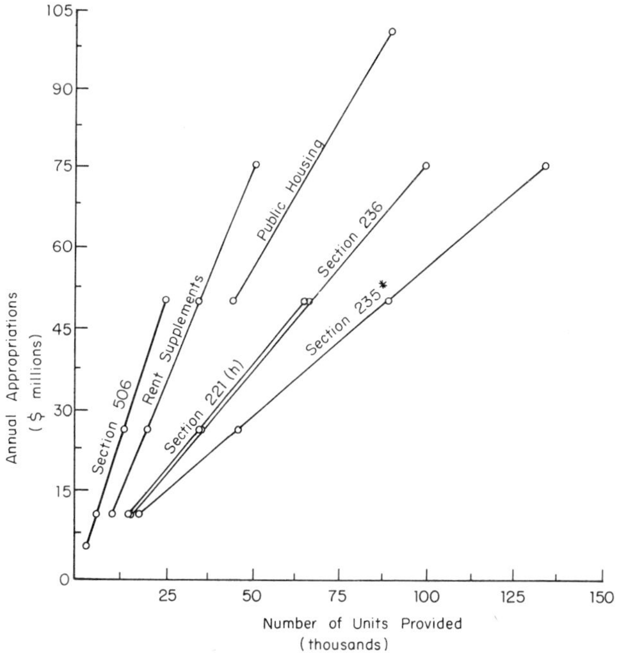

* Based on dwelling cost of $12,500.

ing this maximum annual rent supplement per average unit, for a $10 million appropriation, 5,257 units are provided, representing a 45.3% decrease from the Section 236 BC projections for a given appropriation. To compare these changes with respective changes in other subsidy programs for advantages and disadvantages of each, the various subsidies must be analyzed in detail. Here the subsidy programs' effects will only be detailed as applied to the rehabilitation BC, unless a special relationship exists for the new construction BC.

Section 235 Program

The Section 235 subsidy formula applied to the special rehabilitation BC, assuming a dwelling cost of $12,500, reduces required mortgage payments by 54.1% with a maximum periodic payment of $47 per month, and reduces actual mortgage payments from $87 to $40. With the maximum annual periodic payment per average unit, 17,823 units could be provided for a $10 million appropriation, 22.6% more than Section 236 projections for the same appropriation. This is due primarily to the lower subsidy required, based on the project's decreased development costs.

The low monthly "rent" listed in Table IX is based only on subsidized debt service requirements, excluding all other normal occupancy expenses. The government apparently anticipates that additional expenses can be absorbed by the difference between the 20% of income spent for rent used in Section 235 calculations and the 25% income factor usually applied. Minimum income, based on the 20% factor and the $40 monthly mortgage payment, equals $2,420 per year. The 5% spread in income factors applied to this minimum income amounts to $10 per month, too low to cover other required occupancy expenses, which could total as much as the mortgage payments, depending on the project location and the homeowner's capacity to do his own maintenance and repairs.

The other minimum income listed in Table IX results from the other basis used for calculating the allowable periodic payment; that is, the home owner pays the monthly payment balance due for principal, interest, insurance premium, real estate taxes, and home insurance under the market rate mortgage and 20% of family income. Assuming real estate taxes and home insurance at 2% of original dwelling costs, the breakpoint where this alternative subsidy formula rule takes effect is at $3,670 annual income. Between these two minimum incomes ($2,420 and $3,670 per year) the same maximum periodic payment of

$47 per month applies. The upper limit seems to be the most realistic eligibility requirement. At this level the 5-point spread in income factors would result in a $15 per month surplus for additional occupancy expenses besides the $61 per month allocated to mortgage payments, real estate taxes, and home insurance expenses. This $76 total monthly budget plus the $47 periodic payment equals a $123 total occupancy cost for market conditions. This still seems unrealistic compared with market rents of $173 for the Section 236 rehabilitation BC, but such levels are perhaps feasible for low-cost areas.

It is likely that in practice the Section 235 income levels will be above even the upper limit for minimum incomes, somewhere between the $3,670 level and the $7,075 income maximum. In this event, periodic payments will be reduced accordingly and the units provided will increase. In general, the Section 235 Program is difficult to evaluate because of many unknown factors. Mortgage subsidies and eligibility limits will probably in practice be set by the authorizing agency for each particular circumstance.

Section 221(h) Program

The Section 221(h) subsidy formula applied to the rehabilitation BC reduces required basic rents by 54.1%, and absolute rents from $173 to $113 per month, based on an interest rate subsidy of $60 per month. These absolute rents and subsidy amounts are the same as for the Section 236 subsidy formula applied to BC3. Similarly, the number of units provided for a given appropriation equals the Section 236 projections. However, this comparison is a simplification for several reasons. Under the Section 221(h) subsidy formula, interest is reduced to an effective 1% and basic rents are calculated directly on resulting debt service requirements. This procedure, then, automatically reduces contingencies and other expenses based on total project income. Real estate taxes are also decreased through a negotiated settlement. The Section 236 subsidy formula applies a periodic payment based on the reduced interest rate. Recently issued Section 236 guidelines indicate that the two formulas will operate to the same effect in practice. However, as respective subsidy formulas currently stand, there are significant differences which could influence rents and incomes.

Discrepancies also exist in the projections made. Annual appropriations for the Section 221(h) Program are tied to the outstanding mortgage principal for all projects assisted, because the mortgages under this program are purchased by the government through FNMA. The mortgages may subsequently be discounted, making up the difference between the 1% rate and the market rate, and resold. The purchasing or discounting, however, requires large expenditures at the time of transfer rather than spreading subsidy commitments over the mortgage term by a device similar to the periodic payments. Our calculations assumed that the government's effective cost was equalized over the mortgage term, thereby equating the Section 221(h) and 236 projections. This is a distortion, since under Section 221(h) the government is committed to the 1% rate, or at best to a 3% rate. Under Section 236, periodic payments are adjusted according to tenant incomes until the market rate is reached. Total government commitments are likely to be less for Section 236 than for Section 221(h). The Section 221(h) Program is to be phased out and replaced by Section 235 or 236 as the latter become fully operative.

Rent Supplement Program

The Rent Supplement Program applied to the rehabilitation BC reduces absolute rents from $173 to $52 per month, a $121 monthly subsidy, the maximum allowable supplement payment calculated as 70.0% of market rents. Rent supplements are calculated by applying the applicable subsidy percentage after all occupancy costs are totaled to determine market rents. This program allows great flexibility in setting basic rents in the range from a 70% reduction of market rents. The particular percentage would be established on the basis of 25% of the income of the family to be accommodated. Note also that rent supplements can effectively offset all occupancy costs. Other subsidy formulas aim primarily at reducing debt service requirements through interest rate manipulation and do not affect annual expenses. Rent supplements are especially useful, therefore, in high operating cost areas. Additional benefits are often achieved by combining such supplements with other subsidy programs to reduce rents selectively as required.

Projections for the Rent Supplement Program show a pronounced decrease in the units provided for a given appropriation, 50.4% of Section 236 projections, because of the $121 monthly subsidy amount which is just over twice the Section 236 periodic payment amount. It would be preferable to spread available appropriations over more units by attaching supplements to other subsidy programs. In this way, the supplement itself can be reduced, although rents and incomes remain at the same levels. For example, a $61 per month rent supplement "piggybacked" on the $113 basic Section 236 rent results in a $52 net rent, the same as for a $121 rent supplement applied by itself. In this instance, the number of units provided remains constant (adding the two forms of subsidy and dividing the total amount into assumed appropriations). Surplus rent supplements can be applied to other projects or to other units in greater amounts, however, to meet particular rent and income needs.

Public Housing

The Public Housing subsidy formula applied to the rehabilitation BC reduces rents and incomes by 60.2%, considering both debt service subsidies and real estate tax and contingency allowance reductions, representing an absolute rent decrease from $173 to $69 per month based on a $104 total monthly subsidy. Considering debt service subsidy only, the reduction is 56.2%, decreasing absolute rents to $76 per month with a subsidy amount equal to $97 per month. This latter amount is used to calculate the units provided for a given appropriation, representing the amount of federal contribution. The $7 per month difference between the two subsidy levels results from real estate tax reductions granted by municipal governments and contingency reductions allowed by the management agency. Unfortunately, the new subsidy formulas, such as for Section 236, do not explicitly account for this type of secondary cost reduction.

The units provided under the Public Housing Program reduce 38.1% from Section 236 projections for a given appropriation, owing to the fact that all debt service requirements are subsidized under public housing compared to the maximum decrease to a 1% rate under Section 236. Debt service requirements in our calculations were based on a mortgage with a 6.75% interest rate and a 40-year amortization. Historically, public housing has been financed through municipal bond issues, debt service requirements of which were fully subsidized through annual federal contributions to the Local Housing Authority. These tax-free municipal bonds usually carried interest rates between 3% and 5% and matured for terms up to 50 years or more. These lower rates and longer terms reduced the subsidy requirements for debt servicing. Bond issues, however, were awkward and time-consuming financial devices requiring public hearings or referendums. Thus projects tended to be large developments to take full advantage of issuing bonds. Such large, often isolated projects became unpopular over time. Amendments to the public housing provisions in HUDA 68 respond to these problems by stressing smaller projects built under market mortgage conditions. HUDA 68 also stresses programs involving tenants in project development, management, and services. These are the "Turnkey" programs under which a developer builds housing by normal methods and then turns the completed project over to the local authority. Conventional financing is usually used since it would be difficult to issue bonds for each separate project. In the future, however, a bond device could be created for blanket issues to finance several projects, taking full advantage of lower interest rates possible with municipal bonds and subsequently reducing the amount of debt service subsidy required for a given project. The end result would be allocation of available appropriations to more units.

Section 506 Program

The Section 506 Program applied to the rehabilitation BC reduces rents by 10.9%. The absolute rent reduction is from $173 to $154 per month. The subsidy is a land writedown during the development term, reducing land and building acquisition costs from $2,000 to $1 per unit. This cost saving operates through the cost structure to reduce rents, but it is not translated as a monthly payment as are the interest rate of other subsidies. This subsidy formula's advantage is that it is an integral part of the project, effectively reducing development costs, debt service requirements, and other expenses calculated in terms of total project income. Such lump sum payments, however, require substantial expenditures in a given year rather than annualizing the subsidy over the project life, which reduces the units that can be provided for a given appropriation. This is clearly seen in the projections, where the number of rehabilitated units provided decreases 63.9% from Section 236 BC projections. The Section 506 Program thus seems to have a limited effect on rents and incomes and is not a very efficient subsidy method in terms of units provided. However, land writedown subsidies are useful as a supplementary program, especially in areas where land values are high.

Note also that the reduction in rents and incomes for Section 506 land writedowns applied to the new construction BC is only 4.0% compared with 10.9% for rehabilitation, as a result of the greater original land and building acquisition cost for rehabilitation ($2,000 per unit) compared with the land acquisition cost for new construction ($1,000 per unit). Subsequently, more land writedown subsidies can be

GRAPH 13. NUMBER OF UNITS PROVIDED UNDER OTHER SUBSIDY PROGRAMS (AND SECTION 236 PROGRAM) VS. RENTALS REQUIRED AND INCOME LEVELS SERVED: BY PROGRAM

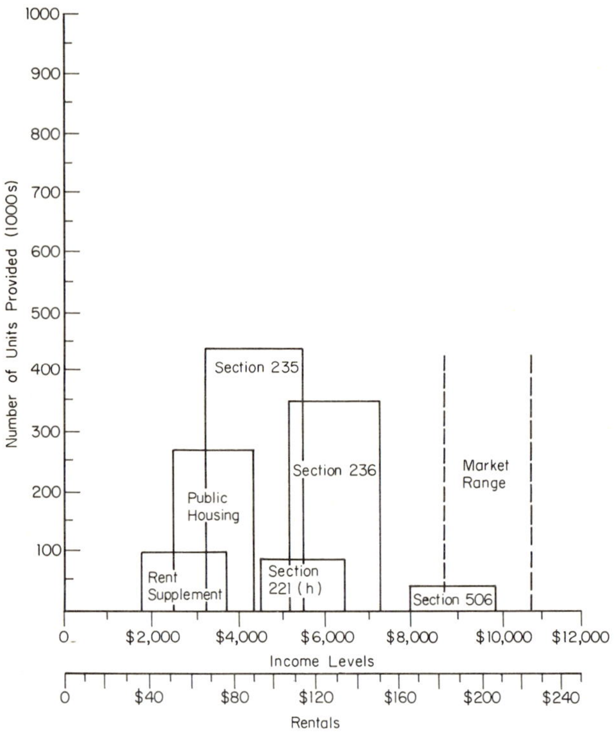

GRAPH 14. NUMBER OF UNITS PROVIDED UNDER OTHER SUBSIDY PROGRAMS (AND SECTION 236 PROGRAM) VS. RENTALS REQUIRED AND INCOME LEVELS SERVED: TOTAL

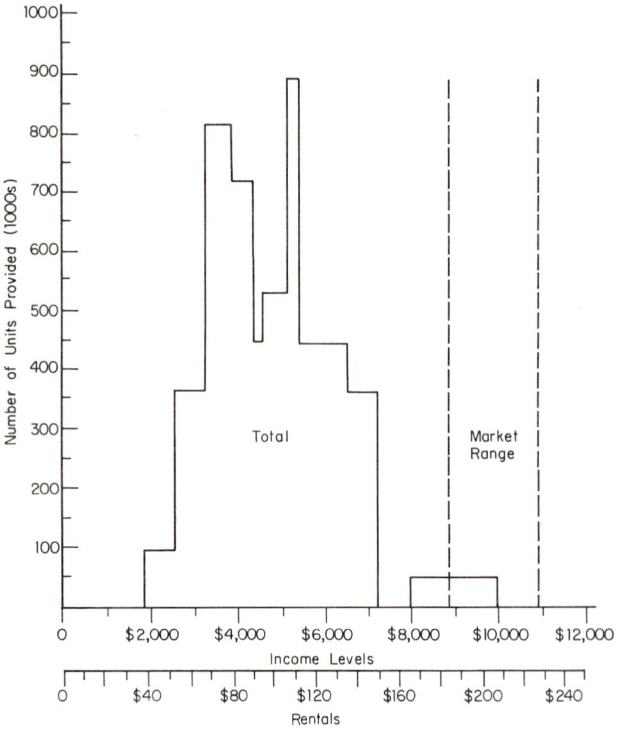

absorbed by the rehabilitation project than by the new construction project, assuming acquisition costs are reduced to $1 per unit in each case. Increased writedown means, however, that more of available appropriations are used for a single project, as can be seen in the projections, where new units increase 4.2% over Section 236 BC projections, while rehabilitated units decrease 63.9%. These trade-offs between reduction in rents and incomes versus the units provided again emphasize the advantages and disadvantages of this form of subsidy.

Summary

Cumulative projections of the units provided can be made for HUDA 68's authorized (not necessarily funded) appropriations, as follows:

Subsidy Program	*Total (or Increased) Annual Appropriation by Fiscal 1971*
Section 236	$300 million
Section 235	300 million
Section 221(h)	50 million
Rent supplements	140 million
Public housing	400 million
Section 506	50 million (hypothetical)

The cumulative projections assume that new construction projects under the respective subsidy formulas establish maximum rents and income levels and that rehabilitation projects establish the minimum. The average subsidy amount for this minimum/maximum range is then divided into the annual appropriations above to determine total units possible under a given program and plotted for an assumed rent spread of ± $20 per month. The results are presented in Graphs 13 and 14, providing a simplified but useful approximation of HUDA 68's impact in terms of the lower-income sectors served. Further evaluations should be made as to how this potential housing supply matches each sector's demand.

It is apparent that overlaps and duplications exist between different subsidy programs. An argument could be made that each program's most effective features should be combined into one all-inclusive program, to simplify procedures for providing proper housing for lower-income families. National housing programs in this country, however, have traditionally been evolutionary. For a variety of reasons, none has ever been sufficient to serve the needs, but the evolution has continued in the right direction. This report presents considerable evidence that HUDA

68 provides the most extensive measures to date. It would be foolish, however, to discard preceding programs prematurely rather than apply all available resources. HUDA 68 anticipates phasing out redundant programs as new provisions become operative, but this process will require some time.

There is no one solution to existing housing problems. A wide range of programs will probably always be required to satisfy particular income sectors and local conditions. It might be that in certain areas the available housing stock is sound but deteriorating, suggesting rehabilitation as the proper approach, while elsewhere, where the stock is poorly adapted to rehabilitation or where open sites exist, new construction may be the better alternative. Similarly, in certain locations home ownership may be the accepted pattern and it would be wrong to impose other standards without good reason. The cost of providing any given type of housing also will vary widely with location. In one area interest rate reductions alone may be sufficient to meet the needs of lower-income families, while in another location it may be that high land costs must be offset by land writedown subsidies, in addition to interest rate subsidies, to make rent reductions effective. In areas of exceptional cost or depressed incomes, rent supplements could be used to reduce basic rents still further.

Many other possible combinations can be applied to achieve the required results. These packages are not neat solutions, but they offer flexible means of responding to the low-income housing market's diversity. HAM provides a technique for analyzing the implications of alternative methods for applying subsidy programs and program combinations to satisfy low-income housing requirements. Only through a comprehensive application of resources determined through rigorous analysis can HUDA 68's objectives be accomplished.

Recapitulation

This report presents an economic analysis of HUDA 68, based on a computer simulation of the major subsidy programs it established. A number of our conclusions should serve as useful guidelines for policy decisions and practical applications.

We considered five cost categories: land costs, construction or rehabilitation costs, debt service (mortgage term and interest rate), expenses, and real estate tax. (A sixth item in the analysis, the rent/income ratio, is really a conversion factor for determining the part of a family's budget to be spent on housing and is not treated here as a cost category.) These cost categories are clearly rather general divisions; the cost structure could be itemized in much greater detail. Construction or rehabilitation costs, for example, could be divided into dwelling structures, site improvements, utility connections, and other fees and charges. The housing structure entry could be itemized into a very detailed list of building materials, labor operations, and overhead. But as the number of categories or details within categories increases, the number of alternative variations correspondingly expands. Another practical consideration is the availability of accurate cost data on such details. At present, relevant cost information is generally available only in aggregated form; that is, construction costs are reported as per square foot or operating expenses as per room per annum. In any event, we assumed that generalized cost categories were sufficient for testing broad policy issues. The results are intended primarily as indications of cost structure sensitivity to selected subsidy program and cost variations, not as calculations of absolute dollar values. HAM, however, can accomplish both types of results and continued efforts are being made to collect the necessary data for accurate, detailed analysis.

Besides the cost categories, calculations are based on numerous explicit and implicit assumptions. Certain of these, such as project size and composition, appropriation levels, and so forth, the procedure states clearly. Other less obvious assumptions, programmed internally in the model, relate the different cost structure variables; that is, they create the mathematical formulas which constitute the simulation model. For example, the program calculates architects' fees based on total construction costs plus builders' fees, and real estate taxes as a percentage of total project income less contingencies. Many of these assumptions are simple arithmetic functions; some are relatively fixed by policy or practice. Others should be considered as variable as the cost categories themselves. Such assumptions represent additional alternatives to be tested, extending the complexity of a thorough analysis.

Each cost category and structural assumption is assigned a typical input value to establish the BC. Variations, usually percentage adjustments of typical costs, are subsequently posited and used for testing the impact of such changes on the project cost structure. In this study we usually compared only four or five alternative cost estimates, but the number of possibilities is unlimited. These variations are performed independently of each other, with only one input value altered at a time and the others held constant. Input values could also be varied interdependently, but this would greatly multiply the number of alternatives to be tested. Such cumulative or combined changes are an important subject of future cost analysis. Results of such cost changes may not be additive; combinations of changes may be more or less than the sum of these changes calculated separately. For instance, an interest rate subsidy piggybacked with a land write-down subsidy not only reduces debt service requirements directly, and hence rent and income levels, but also reduces development costs on which the debt service is calculated. The total effect on rents and incomes, however, may be more or less than the simple compounding of the two subsidies applied separately. Similarly, provisions of the Section 236 and Rent Supplement Programs could legally be combined to good effect, providing each project with a wider range of subsidized rents. Rents of $25 per month are permissible using this combination. Further analysis should investigate the efficacy of such combined subsidy approaches.

HAM, then, involves three types of functions: cost categories or variables, explicit or implicit structural assumptions, and alternative cost estimates. This study employs five cost categories, perhaps ten significant structural assumptions, and up to five alternative estimates, including the base case typical costs. Even if these functions are only varied independently, one at a time, there are approximately three hundred possible combinations to be tested for each subsidy program analyzed. Thus our procedure was necessarily selective. If interdependent variations had also been considered, the alternatives would number in the hundreds of thousands. Because of this inherent complexity of housing cost analysis, and because all the alternatives could not conceivably be anticipated or processed, the simulation model has been designed as an interactive program. The interactive approach allows use of the model for testing specifically defined objectives, entering and varying only the necessary variables, assumptions, and estimates.

This discussion also suggests the attitude with which this study should be received. Although we present specific numerical results in terms of units provided, rentals required, and family income levels served, these results must always be viewed in the framework of the cost variables, assumptions, and estimates underlying each step of the analysis. The results have particular meaning and may be generalized only to the extent that these underlying variables, assumptions, and estimates validly define a housing situation. Every effort has been made to provide accurate and typical results. To reduce possibilities of distortion or misrepresentation, however, the report emphasizes principles and relationships, although these are necessarily illustrated in terms of numerical results. This is also why comparative tables and percentile graphs are used which indicate such principles and relationships somewhat independently from specific results. It is quality rather than quantity of change that is significant in the analysis.

More importantly, perhaps, this study demonstrates a methodology which can ultimately provide a rational basis for both qualitative and quantitative analysis for housing policy formulation. To the best of our knowledge, this is the first use of a computer model for systematic analysis of housing subsidy and cost alternatives. Rule-of-thumb guided by intuition has been the housing industry's typical analytical procedure. Use of a model required that many implicit assumptions and intuitional relationships be made explicit and precise. The methodology therefore has value in itself. Furthermore, as this report illustrates, specific results can be produced with great facility for particular cases.

Additional studies should extend these initial analytical results in both detail and depth. For example, this study developed and tested only four BC projects, although local building conditions vary widely. A more complete analysis would develop many BCs, each with characteristics describing significant variations, which could then be tested for a broad range of alternative cost variables, assumptions, and estimates with results ranked by effectiveness. Cumulative or combined effects of these variations would also be analyzed. Similarly, alternative subsidy programs and combinations of programs could be simulated and compared. HAM can already perform such analysis, and it only remains for objectives to be defined. Let this report be the first step toward comprehensive analysis of the economic aspects of housing for use in policy and program formulation.

Appendix

PROCEDURE AND RESULTS

BASE CASES AND PROFITABILITY ANALYSIS

As Chapter Three made clear, systematic application of HAM to HUDA 68 involves a long series of computer operations. We have organized this series into a sequence of seventeen steps. The first steps establish the four BCs.

Steps 1 and 3: Base Cases

Procedure for nonprofit BCs (BC1 and BC3): The analysis procedure is based on the cost structure diagram shown in Diagram K. The structure's implicit cost variables and assumptions are detailed in the standard input/output data format. Certain inputs are estimated directly (e.g., land and building acquisition cost estimated at $1,000 per unit, operating expenses at $100 per room per annum); others are estimated indirectly as proportions of variables calculated independently (e.g., builder's overhead is taken as 2% of construction or rehabilitation costs, real estate taxes are a percentage of total project income). Once these values and relationships are established, HAM computes all cost values and the appropriate subtotals and totals for the project's development costs and occupancy expenses. (See Diagram C, page 9.) The final output contains these results as well as rents per month for different units and minimum income levels per year for families served by this housing.

Results for nonprofit BCs: Exhibit 1 presents inputs and outputs developed for the new construction and rehabilitation nonprofit sponsored BCs (BC1 and BC3). They are 100-unit projects, with total development costs of $2,215,610 for BC1 and $1,528,243 for BC3. Annual occupancy expenses based on the development cost are $272,026 for BC1 and $206,680 for BC3. Distributions of these results for an average unit are as follows:

Development Cost Category	*Cost Per Unit*		*Percentage of Total Cost*	
	BC1	BC3	BC1	BC3
Land and building acquisition	$ 1,000	$ 2,000	4.5%	13.1%
Construction or rehabilitation cost	16,404	10,000	74.1	65.5
Development fees	2,493	1,657	11.2	10.8
Carrying and financing charges	2,259	1,625	10.2	10.6
Total	$22,156	$15,282	100.0%	100.0%

Occupancy Expense Category	*Expense per Unit*		*Percentage of Total Cost*	
	BC1	BC3	BC1	BC3
Debt service and profit	$ 1,724	$ 1,190	63.5%	57.7%
Other expenses	996	877	36.5	42.3
Total	$ 2,720	$ 2,067	100.0%	100.0%

DIAGRAM K
COST STRUCTURE, NEW CONSTRUCTION AND REHABILITATION, NONPROFIT (BC1 AND BC3)

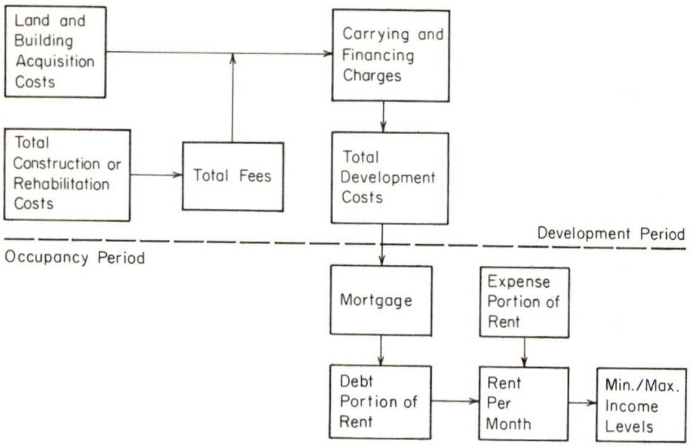

Monthly market rentals necessary to make these projects economically feasible range for BC1 from $158 for a one-bedroom unit to $294 for a four-bedroom unit, and from $120 to $223 for similar BC3 units. (Rents are calculated first on a per room per month basis, then allocated to each unit type according to total number of rooms per unit.)

Minimum family incomes equivalent to these rentals range from $7,600 to $14,100 per year, respectively, for BC1, and from $5,800 to $10,750 for BC3. Considering allowances established by the Federal Housing Administration (FHA), maximum incomes range for BC1 from $8,000 to $16,800 per year and for BC3 from $6,100 to $13,200. The average BC1 rent and income levels are $227 and $10,900; for BC3, $173 and $8,300.

EXHIBIT 1. COST VARIABLES, ASSUMPTIONS, AND ESTIMATES: NEW CONSTRUCTION, NONPROFIT (BC1)

Land Acquisition Costs		
$1,000 per unit × 100 units		$ 100,000
Construction Costs		
(including housing structure, utility connection, site develment, bond premiums, and quantity survey)		
12 one bedroom (3.5 room) units @ $11,950 per unit	$143,400	
38 two " (4.5 room) " @ 14,900 " "	566,000	
38 three " (5.5 room) " @ 17,900 " "	680,000	
12 four " (6.5 room) " @ 20,900 " "	251,000	
Total		$1,640,400
Development Fees		
Builder's overhead @ 2.00% of construction costs	$ 32,800	
Builder's profit @ 4.75% " " "	78,000	
Builder's and sponsor's profit and risk allowance @ —% of estimated development cost	—	
Architect's fees @ 4.75% (design fee) plus 1.50% (supervision fee) of construction costs and builder's fees	105,000	
Housing consultant	23,500	
Legal fees and organizational costs	10,000	
Total		$ 249,300
Carrying and Financing Charges		
Interest during 12 month construction period @ 6.75% on average loan of $1,110,000	$ 74,925	
Property taxes	10,000	
Insurance	5,000	
FHA examination fee @ 0.3% of estimated mortgage amount	6,516	
FHA inspection fee @ 0.5% " " " "	10,861	
Financing expenses @ 3.0% " " " "	65,165	
Working capital @ 2.0% " " " "	43,443	
Title and recording costs	10,000	
Total		$ 225,910
Total Development Costs		$2,215,610

EXHIBIT 1, CONTINUED

Mortgage Amount (100% of total development costs)		$2,215,610
Equity Investment		$ —
Annual Debt Service and Profit Requirements (level annuity payments for year 1)		
Interest payments (6.75% interest rate)	$149,554	
Amortization payments (40 year mortgage term)	11,835	
Mortgage premiums (0.5% FHA insurance premium)	11,077	
Limited-dividend distributions (—% profit on equity)	—	
Total		$ 172,466
Annual Expenses		
Operating expenses (including administration, operation, maintenance, decorating reserve, and replacement reserve) @ $100 per room per annum	$ 50,100	
Real estate taxes (10% rate on total project income)	24,730	
Vacancy and collection loss plus 5% contingencies	24,730	
Total		$ 99,560
Total Occupancy Expenses		$ 272,026
Required Annual Charges Per Average BC1 Unit	$ 2,720	
Debt service and profit portion	1,724	
Expense portion	996	

REQUIRED MONTHLY CHARGES PER UNIT AND EQUIVALENT ANNUAL FAMILY INCOMES

Number of Bedrooms	*Market Rents (per month)*	*Minimum Income Levels * (per year)*	*Maximum Income ** Levels (per year)*
1	$158	$ 7,607	$ 8,008
2	204	9,781	10,927
3	249	11,955	13,847
4	294	14,128	16,767
per average unit	227	10,896	
per room	45		

* Based on 25% of net family income to be paid for rent.

** Based on 25% of gross family income to be paid for rent. Net income is taken as 95% of gross family income less $300 per child under 21 years of age. The number of deductions for children is limited by the size of the dwelling unit as follows:

Number of Bedrooms	*Number of Allowable Deductions*
1	0
2	2
3	4
4	6

EXHIBIT 1, CONTINUED. COST VARIABLES, ASSUMPTIONS, AND ESTIMATES: REHABILITATION, NONPROFIT (BC3)

Land and Building Acquisition Costs		
$2,000 per unit × 100 units		$ 200,000
Rehabilitation Costs (including housing structure, utility connection, site development, bond premiums, and quantity survey)		
12 one bedroom (3.5 room) units @ $ 7,300 per unit	$ 87,500	
38 two " (4.5 room) " @ 9,400 " "	345,000	
38 three " (5.5 room) " @ 10,900 " "	414,500	
12 four " (6.5 room) " @ 12,750 " "	153,000	
Total		$1,000,000
Development Fees		
Builder's overhead @ 2.00% of construction costs	$ 20,000	
Builder's profit @ 4.75% " " "	47,500	
Builder's and sponsor's profit and risk allowance @ –% of estimated development cost	—	
Architect's fees @ 4.75% (design fee) plus 1.50% (supervision fee) of construction costs and builder's fees	66,718	
Housing consultant	23,500	
Legal fees and organizational costs	8,000	
Total		$ 165,718
Carrying and Financing Charges		
Interest during 12 month construction period @ 6.75% on average loan of $750,000	$ 50,625	
Property taxes	10,000	
Insurance	5,000	
FHA examination fee @ 0.3% of estimated mortgage amount	4,495	
FHA inspection fee @ 0.5% " " " "	7,491	
Financing expenses @ 3.0% " " " "	44,948	
Working capital @ 2.0% " " " "	29,966	
Title and recording costs	10,000	
Total		$ 162,525
Total Development Costs		$1,528,243

EXHIBIT 1, CONTINUED

Mortgage Amount (100% of total development costs)		$1,528,243
Equity Investment		$ —
Annual Debt Service and Profit Requirements (level annuity payments for year 1)		
Interest payments (6.75% interest rate)	$103,136	
Amortization payments (40 year mortgage term)	8,163	
Mortgage premiums (0.5% FHA insurance premium)	7,711	
Limited-dividend distributions (—% profit on equity)	—	
Total		$ 119,010
Annual Expenses		
Operating expenses (including administration, operation, maintenance, decorating reserve, and replacement reserve) @ $100 per room per annum	$ 50,100	
Real estate taxes (10% rate on total project income)	18,785	
Vacancy and collection loss plus 5% contingencies	18,785	
Total		$ 87,670
Total Occupancy Expenses		$ 206,680
Required Annual Charges Per Average BC3 Unit	$ 2,067	
Debt service and profit portion	1,190	
Expense portion	877	

REQUIRED MONTHLY CHARGES PER UNIT AND EQUIVALENT ANNUAL FAMILY INCOMES

Number of Bedrooms	*Market Rents (per month)*	*Minimum Income Levels * (per year)*	*Maximum Income Levels ** (per year)*
1	$120	$ 5,791	$ 6,096
2	155	7,446	8,470
3	189	9,101	10,843
4	223	10,755	13,216
per average unit	173	8,304	
per room	34		

* Based on 25% of net family income to be paid for rent.

** Based on 25% of gross family income to be paid for rent. Net income is taken as 95% of gross family income less $300 per child under 21 years of age. The number of deductions for children is limited by the size of the dwelling unit as follows:

Number of Bedrooms	*Number of Allowable Deductions*
1	0
2	2
3	4
4	6

Procedure for limited-dividend BCs (BC2 and BC4): The nonprofit BC general procedure also applies for the limited-dividend alternative, with certain specific characteristics modified consistent with the organizational and financing differences of limited-dividend projects. These changes are:

- The builder's profit is eliminated as a separate cost variable, and a builder's and sponsor's profit and risk allowance is substituted. This allowance is fixed at 9.5% of the total development costs.
- The BC2 construction loan is reduced to $1,012,000 on the assumption that the sponsor will finance part of the development costs.
- The housing consultant fee and the working capital provisions are eliminated as separate variables since these costs are absorbed by the sponsor directly.
- The sponsor's equity is set as 10% of total development cost. The sponsor is allowed a 6% annual return on this equity. (Technically, the return is calculated as 6% of 11.11% of the mortgage amount.)

The simulation model subsequently computes new outputs for development costs, debt service, profit requirements, occupancy expenses, rental charges, and income levels generated by these project characteristics. These costs are shown below.

Development Cost Category	*Cost per Unit*		*% of Total Cost*	
	BC2	BC4	BC2	BC4
Land acquisition	$ 1,000	$ 2,000	4.4%	12.9%
Construction costs	16,404	10,000	73.0	64.4
Development fees	3,385	2,240	15.0	14.4
Carrying and financing charges	1,714	1,295	7.6	8.3
Total	$22,503	$15,535	100.0%	100.0%

Occupancy Expense Category	*Expense per Unit*		*% of Total Expense*	
	BC2	BC4	BC2	BC4
Debt service and profit	$ 1,712	$ 1,181	63.6%	57.8%
Other expenses	976	864	36.4	42.2
Total	$ 2,688	$ 2,045	100.0%	100.0%

Results for limited-dividend BCs: Exhibit 2 presents the inputs and outputs developed for the limited-dividend BCs.

BC2's total development cost is $2,250,339 and annual occupancy expenses are $268,772; the BC4 project costs $1,553,517 and $204,557, respectively. Distribution of these results for an average unit is given above.

Monthly market rentals required to make the project economically feasible range for BC2 from $156 for a one bedroom unit to $291 for a four bedroom unit, with a $224 average; for BC4 the respective range is $119 to $221, averaging $170. Minimum BC2 family incomes for these rentals are $7,500 and $13,950 per year, respectively, with an average of $10,750; with standard allowances, the maximum incomes range from $7,900 to $16,600 per year. For BC4 the corresponding figures range from $5,700 to $10,600, averaging $8,200, with maximums ranging from $6,000 to $13,050.

EXHIBIT 2. COST VARIABLES, ASSUMPTIONS, AND ESTIMATES: NEW CONSTRUCTION, LIMITED-DIVIDEND (BC2)

Land Acquisition Costs		
$1,000 per unit × 100 units		$ 100,000
Construction Costs (*including housing structure, utility connection, site development, bond premiums, and quantity survey*)		
12 one bedroom (3.5 room) units @ $11,950 per unit	$143,400	
38 two " (4.5 room) " @ 14,900 " "	566,000	
38 three " (5.5 room) " @ 17,900 " "	680,000	
12 four " (6.5 room) " @ 20,900 " "	251,000	
Total		$1,640,400
Development Fees		
Builder's overhead @ 2.00% of construction costs	$ 32,800	
Builder's profit @ —% " " "	—	
Builder and sponsor's profit and risk allowance @ 9.5% of estimated development cost	195,235	
Architect's fees @ 4.75% (design fee) plus 1.50% (supervision fee) of construction costs and builder's fees	100,500	
Housing consultant	—	
Legal fees and organizational costs	10,000	
Total		$ 338,535
Carrying and Financing Charges		
Interest during 12 month construction period @ 6.75% on average loan of $1,012,000	$ 68,310	
Property taxes	10,000	
Insurance	5,000	
FHA examination fee @ 0.3% of estimated mortgage amount	6,165	
FHA inspection fee @ 0.5% " " " "	10,276	
Financing expenses @ 3.0% " " " "	61,653	
Working capital @ —% " " " "	—	
Title and recording costs	10,000	
Total		$ 171,404
Total Development Costs		$2,250,339
Mortgage Amount (90% of total development costs)		$2,025,305
Equity Investment		$ 225,034
Annual Debt Service and Profit Requirements (level annuity payments for year 1)		
Interest payments (6.75% interest rate)	$136,708	
Amortization payments (40 year mortgage term)	10,818	
Mortgage premiums (0.5% FHA insurance premium)	10,126	
Limited-dividend distributions (6.0% profit on equity)	13,502	
		$ 171,154
Annual Expenses		
Operating expenses (including administration, operation, maintenance, decorating reserve, and replacement reserve) @ $100 per room per annum	$ 50,100	
Real estate taxes (10% rate on total project income)	23,084	
Vacancy and collection loss plus 5% contingencies	24,434	
Total		$ 97,618
Total Occupancy Expenses		$ 268,772

EXHIBIT 2. CONTINUED. COST VARIABLES, ASSUMPTIONS, AND ESTIMATES: REHABILITATION, LIMITED-DIVIDEND (BC4)

Land and Building Acquisition Costs		
$2,000 per unit × 100 units		$ 200,000
Rehabilitation Costs (including housing structure, utility connection, site development, bond premiums, and quantity survey)		
12 one bedroom (3.5 room) units @ $ 7,300 per unit	$ 87,500	
38 two " (4.5 room) " @ 9,100 " "	345,000	
38 three " (5.5 room) " @ 10,900 " "	414,500	
12 four " (6.5 room) " @ 12,750 " "	153,000	
Total		1,000,000
Development Fees		
Builder's overhead @ 2.00% of construction costs	$ 20,000	
Builder's profit @ —% " " "	—	
Builder's and sponsor's profit and risk allowance @ 9.5% of estimated development cost	134,780	
Architect's fees @ 4.75% (design fee) plus 1.50% (supervision fee) of construction costs and builder's fees	61,200	
Housing consultant	—	
Legal fees and organizational costs	8,000	
Total		$ 223,980
Carrying and Financing Charges		
Interest during 12 month construction period @ 6.75% on average loan of $750,000	$ 50,625	
Property taxes	10,000	
Insurance	5,000	
FHA examination fee @ 0.3% of estimated development costs	4,256	
FHA inspection fee @ 0.5% " " " "	7,094	
Financing expenses @ 3.0% " " " "	42,562	
Working capital @ —% " " " "	—	
Title and recording costs	10,000	
Total		$ 129,537
Total Development Costs		$1,553,517
Mortgage Amount (90% of total development costs)		$1,398,165
Equity Investment		$ 155,352
Annual Debt Service and Profit Requirements (level annuity payments for year 1)		
Interest payments (6.75% interest rate)	$94,376	
Amortization payments (40 year mortgage term)	7,468	
Mortgage premiums (0.5% FHA insurance premium)	6,991	
Limited-dividend distributions (6.0% profit on equity)	9,321	
Total		$ 118,156
Annual Expenses		
Operating expenses (including administration, operation, maintenance, decorating reserve, and replacement reserve) @ $100 per room per annum	$50,100	
Real estate taxes (10% rate on total project income)	17,659	
Vacancy and collection loss plus 5% contingencies	18,592	
Total		$ 86,351
Total Occupancy Expenses		$ 204,507

EXHIBIT 2, CONTINUED. COST VARIABLES, ASSUMPTIONS, AND ESTIMATES: NEW CONSTRUCTION AND REHABILITATION (BC2 AND BC4)

	BC2	BC4
Required Annual Charges Per Average Unit	$2,688	$2,045
Debt service and profit portion	1,712	1,181
Expense portion	976	864

REQUIRED MONTHLY CHARGES PER UNIT AND EQUIVALENT ANNUAL FAMILY INCOMES

Number of Bedrooms	*Market Rents (per month)*		*Minimum * Income Levels (per year)*		*Maximum ** Income Levels (per year)*	
	BC2	BC4	BC2	BC4	BC2	BC4
1	$156	$119	$ 7,511	$ 5,715	$ 7,906	$ 6,016
2	201	153	9,656	7,348	10,796	8,366
3	246	187	11,802	8,980	13,687	10,716
4	291	221	13,948	10,613	16,577	13,066
per average unit	224	170	10,751	8,180		
per room	45	34				

* Based on 25% of net family income to be paid for rent.

** Based on 25% of gross family income to be paid for rent. Net income is taken as 95% of gross family income less $300 per child under 21 years of age. The number of deductions for children is limited by the size of the dwelling unit as follows:

Number of Bedrooms	*Number of Allowable Deductions*
1	0
2	2
3	4
4	6

Table A–1. Interest and Amortization: New Construction, Limited-Dividend (BC2)

Year	Interest Payments	Amortization Payments	Mortgage Balance	Cumulative Equity	Average Equity
0	0	0	$2,025,305	$225,034	$225,034
1	$136,708	$ 10,818	2,014,487	235,852	230,443
2	135,978	11,548	2,002,938	247,401	236,096
3	135,198	12,328	1,990,611	259,728	242,004
4	134,366	13,160	1,977,450	272,889	248,181
5	133,478	14,048	1,963,402	286,937	254,640
6	132,530	14,997	1,948,405	301,934	261,396
7	131,517	16,009	1,932,397	317,942	268,465
8	130,437	17,089	1,915,307	335,032	275,861
9	129,283	18,243	1,897,064	353,275	283,602
10	128,052	19,474	1,877,590	372,749	291,707
11	126,737	20,789	1,856,801	393,538	300,193
12	125,334	22,192	1,834,608	415,731	309,080
13	123,836	23,690	1,810,918	439,421	318,390
14	122,237	25,289	1,785,629	464,710	328,145
15	120,530	26,996	1,758,633	491,706	338,367
16	118,708	28,819	1,729,814	520,525	349,083
17	116,762	30,764	1,699,050	551,289	360,316
18	114,686	32,840	1,666,210	584,129	372,096
19	112,469	35,057	1,631,153	619,186	384,450
20	110,103	37,423	1,593,729	656,610	397,410
21	107,577	39,950	1,553,780	696,559	411,008
22	104,880	42,646	1,511,134	739,205	425,277
23	102,002	45,525	1,465,609	784,730	440,255
24	98,929	48,598	1,417,011	833,328	455,978
25	95,648	51,878	1,365,133	885,206	472,486
26	92,147	55,380	1,309,754		
27	88,408	59,118	1,250,636		
28	84,418	63,108	1,187,527		
29	80,158	67,368	1,120,159		
30	75,611	71,916	1,048,244		
31	70,756	76,770	971,474		
32	65,574	81,952	889,522		
33	60,043	87,484	802,039		
34	54,138	93,389	708,650		
35	47,834	99,692	608,957		
36	41,105	106,422	502,536		
37	33,921	113,605	388,931		
38	26,253	121,273	267,657		
39	18,067	129,067	138,198		
40	9,328	138,198	0		

Procedure and results for limited-dividend profitability: A HAM subroutine calculates the BC2's sponsor's return on equity according to four profit criteria, and the net present value of all project cash flows. This profitability analysis, it will be recalled, follows a five-stage sequence:

(1) Annual interest and amortization are calculated assuming yearly level annuity payments. The mortgage balance at year's end and the average equity (the average of both original and accrued equity) are also determined. This schedule, shown in Table A-1, is based on an initial $2,025,305 mortgage amount at a 6.75% interest rate, for a 40-year term. The original equity investment is $225,034.

(2) Allowable depreciation deductions for tax purposes are calculated for each year as well as the project's undepreciated balance. (Zero salvage value was assumed.) Any conventional depreciation method can be applied. The 200% double-declining balance method is used here with an automatic shift to the straight-line method when advisable. The accumulated difference between the accelerated and straight-line depreciation method is also determined for use in the capital gains subroutine that follows. Table A-2 shows the schedule resulting from these calculations. It has been assumed that all project costs except land are depreciable over a 25-year life.

TABLE A–2. DEPRECIATION: NEW CONSTRUCTION, LIMITED-DIVIDEND (BC2)

Year	*Depreciation Deduction*	*Undepreciated Balance*	*Accumulated Difference*
0	0	$2,150,339	0
1	$172,027	1,978,312	$ 86,014
2	158,265	1,820,047	158,265
3	145,604	1,674,443	217,855
4	133,955	1,540,488	265,797
5	123,239	1,417,249	303,022
6	113,380	1,303,869	330,389
7	104,310	1,199,559	348,685
8	95,965	1,103,595	358,636
9	88,288	1,015,307	360,910
10	81,225	934,082	356,121
11	74,727	859,356	344,834
12	68,748	790,607	327,569
13	63,249	727,359	304,804
14	60,613	666,746	279,404
15	60,613	606,132	254,003
16	60,613	545,519	228,603
17	60,613	484,906	203,203
18	60,613	424,293	177,802
19	60,613	363,679	152,402
20	60,613	303,066	127,002
21	60,613	242,453	101,601
22	60,613	181,840	76,201
23	60,613	121,226	50,801
24	60,613	60,613	25,400
25	60,613	0	0

(3) Based on the information developed in stages 1 and 2, the project's tax position and cash flows are determined. Additional assumptions are:

- Taxable operating (before-tax) income equals gross revenue less depreciation, interest, and deductible annual expenses, the latter estimated at an average of $97,618.
- After-tax income is equal to the taxable operating income less taxes paid. A tax rate of 52% is assumed.
- If the project should generate a negative after-tax income, a tax saving would result equal to the taxable operating income times the tax rate. It is assumed that the sponsor has other income to shield by the tax savings in the current year.
- The total cash flow equals the 6% limited-dividend distribution on the original equity investment plus any tax savings or less any taxes that result.

On these assumptions, taxable and after-tax incomes and total cash flow, subdivided into taxes paid or tax savings and limited-dividend distribution, are calculated for each year and are shown in Table A–3. Definitions of these terms are given below.

Total Project Revenue

less: Annual Expenses
Depreciation Deduction
Interest Charges
Real Estate Taxes

Taxable Operating Income

less: Taxes Paid or plus: Taxes Saved

After-Tax Income

Total Cash Flow = Taxes Paid or Saved + 6% Limited-Dividend Distribution

(4) The capital gains position resulting from project sale at the end of any year during the first 25 years is determined. Capital gains profit is defined as selling price less capital gains tax and less outstanding mortgage principal at the time of sale. Selling price is assumed to be $2,250,339, the initial purchase price based on development costs. The sponsor's marginal income tax bracket is taken as 52%. The schedule in Table A–4 results from calculations which duplicate Section 1231 (which distinguishes between real estate transactions for trade or business and production of income or investment) and Section 1250 (depreciation recapture rule for real estate) and the Cohn Rule (depreciation in the year of sale may be disallowed) of the Internal Revenue Code.

TABLE A–3. CASH FLOWS:
NEW CONSTRUCTION, LIMITED-DIVIDEND (BC2)

Year	*Before-tax Income*	*After-tax Income**	*Taxes*	*Limited-Dividend Distributions*	*Total Cash Flow*
1	−$147,689	−$76,798	0	$13,502	$90,300
2	−133,197	−69,262	0	13,502	82,764
3	−119,756	−62,273	0	13,502	75,775
4	−107,276	−55,783	0	13,502	69,285
5	−95,671	−49,749	0	13,502	63,251
6	−84,864	−44,129	0	13,502	57,631
7	−74,781	−38,886	0	13,502	52,388
8	−65,356	−33,985	0	13,502	47,487
9	−56,325	−29,393	0	13,502	42,895
10	−48,230	−25,080	0	13,502	38,582
11	−40,418	−21,017	0	13,502	34,515
12	−33,037	−17,179	0	13,502	30,681
13	−26,039	−13,540	0	13,502	27,042
14	−21,804	−11,338	0	13,502	24,840
15	−20,097	−10,451	0	13,502	23,953
16	−18,275	−9,503	0	13,502	23,005
17	−16,330	−8,491	0	13,502	21,993
18	−14,253	−7,412	0	13,502	20,914
19	−12,036	−6,259	0	13,502	19,761
20	−9,670	−5,028	0	13,502	18,530
21	−7,144	−3,715	0	13,502	17,217
22	−4,447	−2,313	0	13,502	15,815
23	−1,569	−816	0	13,502	14,318
24	+1,504	+782	$ 722	13,502	12,720
25	+4,785	+2,488	1,297	13,502	11,998

* If the before-tax income is negative a tax savings results. This is shown as a negative amount. If the before-tax income is positive, the after-tax income is equal to (1–Tax Rate) times the before-tax income. This is shown as a positive amount.

(5) The results generated in stages 1 through 4 are combined to establish four profitability measures:

$$\text{Average after-tax return on equity} = \frac{\text{Average after-tax income}^{1}}{\text{Equity investment}} \quad (1)$$

$$\text{Average cash flow return on equity} = \frac{\text{Average cash flow}}{\text{Equity investment}} \quad (2)$$

$$\text{Average after-tax} + \text{capital gains inflow return on equity} = \frac{\text{Average after-tax income} + \text{capital gains profit}}{\text{Equity investment}} \quad (3)$$

$$\text{Average cash flow} + \text{capital gains inflow return on equity} = \frac{\text{Average cash flow} + \text{capital gains profit}}{\text{Equity investment}} \quad (4)$$

[1] The results shown in Table A–5 are computed using the absolute value of the average after-tax income. If the taxable operating income is negative, a tax savings results. If the before-tax income is positive, the after-tax income is equal to (1-Tax Rate) times the taxable income.

The average after-tax and the average cash flow return on equity criteria apply during each year of the holding period. These criteria with the capital gains inflow added apply in the event of sale at the end of a given year. Although the sponsor's average equity increases over time by an amount equivalent to the amortization payments, we have assumed that the net benefit of these will accrue to the sponsor at the time of sale. They are appropriately considered in the capital gains calculations.

TABLE A–4. CAPITAL GAINS PROFITS: NEW CONSTRUCTION, LIMITED-DIVIDEND (BC2)

Year	*Capital Gains Tax*	*Capital Gains Cash Inflow*
1	$ 89,454	$146,398
2	123,595	123,805
3	168,384	91,345
4	204,134	68,755
5	232,362	54,575
6	254,436	47,498
7	271,587	46,355
8	284,926	50,106
9	295,451	57,823
10	304,064	68,685
11	322,746	70,793
12	339,933	75,798
13	355,745	83,676
14	370,898	93,812
15	386,052	105,655
16	401,205	119,320
17	416,358	134,930
18	431,512	152,617
19	446,665	172,521
20	461,818	194,791
21	476,972	219,588
22	492,125	247,080
23	507,278	277,452
24	522,431	310,896
25	537,585	347,621

The project's present value is also determined for both the holding period and sale conditions. Net present value equals the sum of all project cash inflows and outflows discounted back to year 0. A sponsor's discount rate of 15% is used for these calculations. These profitability criteria and present values for the limited-dividend sponsored project are given in Table A–5.

No separate sponsor's profitability analysis is performed for BC4. The procedure would be the same as for the sponsor's profitability calculated in Step 1, and the results would vary only slightly in magnitude.

GRAPH A–1. CHANGE IN AVERAGE RENT VS. CHANGE IN LAND AND BUILDING ACQUISITION COSTS: NEW CONSTRUCTION AND REHABILITATION, NONPROFIT (BC1 AND BC3)

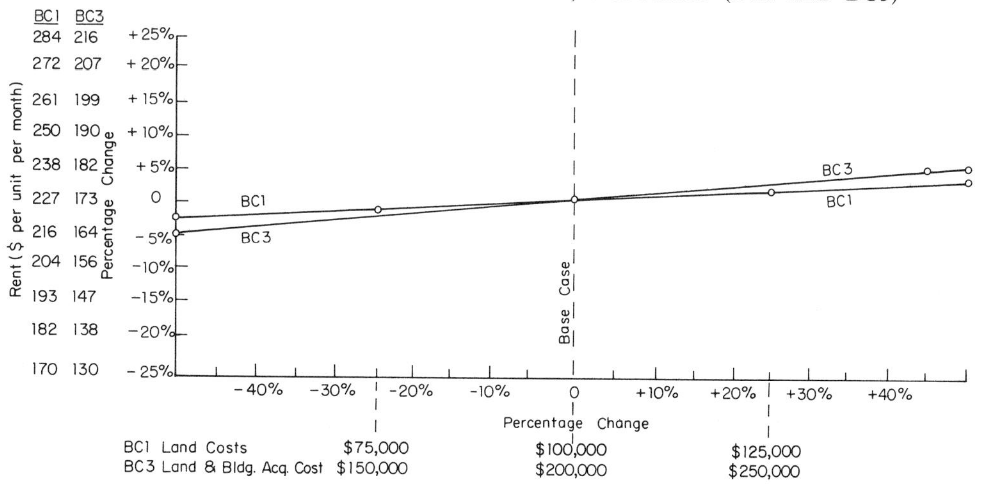

TABLE A–5. PROFITABILITY AND PRESENT VALUE: NEW CONSTRUCTION, LIMITED-DIVIDEND (BC2)

	During Holding Period			*If Sale at End of Year*	
Year	*Average After-tax Return on Equity*	*Average Cash Flow Return on Equity*	*Net Present Value (@ 15%)*	*Average Cash Flow and Capital Gains Inflow Return on Equity*	*Net Present Value (@ 15%)*
0	0.0000	0.0000	−$225,034	0.0000	−$225,034
1	0.3413	0.4013	−151,082	1.0519	−19,194
2	0.3246	0.3846	−92,475	0.6597	9,713
3	0.3087	0.3687	−46,108	0.5039	25,995
4	0.2935	0.3535	−9,499	0.4299	44,869
5	0.2790	0.3390	19,335	0.3875	64,147
6	0.2652	0.3252	41,978	0.3604	82,471
7	0.2520	0.3120	59,696	0.3415	99,065
8	0.2394	0.2994	73,502	0.3272	113,547
9	0.2273	0.2873	84,201	0.3159	125,803
10	0.2157	0.2757	92,439	0.3063	135,885
11	0.2046	0.2646	98,729	0.2932	141,547
12	0.1939	0.2539	103,481	0.2820	146,236
13	0.1837	0.2437	107,021	0.2722	150,066
14	0.1741	0.2341	109,789	0.2639	153,238
15	0.1656	0.2256	112,087	0.2569	155,910
16	0.1579	0.2179	113,984	0.2511	158,137
17	0.1509	0.2109	115,539	0.2461	159,970
18	0.1443	0.2043	116,804	0.2420	161,455
19	0.1382	0.1982	117,823	0.2385	162,634
20	0.1324	0.1924	118,634	0.2357	163,547
21	0.1269	0.1869	119,270	0.2333	164,228
22	0.1216	0.1816	119,758	0.2315	164,708
23	0.1165	0.1765	120,122	0.2301	165,015
24	0.1115	0.1715	120,382	0.2290	165,174
25	0.1066	0.1666	120,557	0.2284	165,209

Steps 2 and 4: Variable Testing for Nonprofit Base Cases

These steps change the estimated values of major cost categories for the BCs established in Steps 1 and 3, to demonstrate the BC cost structure's sensitivity to the selected variations. Results of these systematic changes in each cost category are reported below and in the accompanying tables and graphs. The variable testing in these steps is performed with changes in only one variable at a time, although HAM could also calculate the effects of combined variations.

Changes in land and building acquisition costs: Changes in rentals and income levels resulting from land acquisition cost changes are summarized below and shown in detail in Table A–6. The relationship between rent per average unit and cost of land and building acquisition is plotted in Graph A–1 offering a means to determine quickly the impact of land cost changes.

Percentage Change in Land Cost	*Absolute Value of Land Cost*		*Average Rent per Unit per Month*	
	BC1	BC3	BC1	BC3
−50%	$ 50,000	$100,000	$223	$164
−25	75,000	150,000	225	169
BC 0	100,000	200,000	227	173
+25	125,000	250,000	229	177
+50	150,000	300,000	231	181

TABLE A-6. LAND COSTS:
NEW CONSTRUCTION AND REHABILITATION, NONPROFIT (BC1 AND BC3)

Number of Bedrooms	*Market Rents (per month)*		*Minimum Income Levels (per year)*		*Maximum Income Levels (per year)*	
	BC1	BC3	BC1	BC3	BC1	BC3
A. LAND COSTS (–50%) BC1 = $50,000, BC3 = $100,000						
1	$156	$115	$ 7,467	$ 5,510	$ 7,860	$ 5,800
2	200	148	9,600	7,084	10,737	8,088
3	244	180	11,733	8,658	13,614	10,377
4	289	213	13,866	10,232	16,491	12,665
per avg. unit	223	164	10,688	7,887		
per room	44	33				
B. LAND COSTS (–25%) BC1 = $75,000, BC3 = $150,000						
1	$157	$118	$ 7,537	$ 5,650	$ 7,934	$ 5,948
2	202	151	9,690	7,265	10,832	8,279
3	247	185	11,844	8,879	13,730	10,610
4	292	219	13,997	10,494	16,629	12,941
per avg. unit	225	169	10,789	8,088		
per room	45	34				
C. LAND COSTS (+25%) BC1 = $125,000, BC3 = $250,000						
1	$160	$124	$ 7,678	$ 5,932	$ 8,082	$ 6,245
2	206	159	9,972	7,627	11,023	8,660
3	251	194	12,065	9,322	13,964	11,076
4	297	230	14,259	11,017	16,904	13,492
per avg. unit	229	177	10,990	8,492		
per room	46	35				
D. LAND COSTS (+50%) BC1 = $150,000, BC3 = $300,000						
1	$161	$127	$ 7,748	$ 6,073	$ 8,156	$ 6,393
2	208	163	9,962	7,809	11,118	8,851
3	254	199	12,176	9,544	14,080	11,309
4	300	235	14,390	11,279	17,042	13,767
per avg. unit	231	181	11,091	8,694		
per room	46	36				

TABLE A–7. CONSTRUCTION AND REHABILITATION COSTS: NEW CONSTRUCTION AND REHABILITATION, NONPROFIT (BC1 AND BC3)

Number of Bedrooms	Market Rents (per month)		Minimum Income Levels (per year)		Maximum Income Levels (per year)	
	BC1	BC3	BC1	BC3	BC1	BC3
A. CONSTR.-REHAB. COSTS (−30%) BC1 = $1,148,280, BC3 = $700,000						
1	$126	$101	$ 6,050	$ 4,833	$ 6,368	$ 5,087
2	162	129	7,778	6,214	8,819	7,172
3	198	158	9,507	7,594	11,270	9,257
4	234	187	11,235	8,975	13,720	11,342
per avg. unit	180	144	8,660	6,918		
per room	36	29				
B. CONSTR.-REHAB. COSTS (+10%) BC1 = $1,804,440, BC3 = $1,100,000						
1	$169	$127	$ 8,125	$ 6,110	$ 8,552	$ 6,431
2	218	164	10,446	7,855	11,627	8,900
3	266	200	12,767	9,601	14,702	11,369
4	314	236	15,088	11,347	17,777	13,838
per avg. unit	242	182	11,630	8,746		
per room	48	36				
C. CONSTR.-REHAB. COSTS (+20%) BC1 = $1,968,480, BC3 = $1,200,000						
1	$180	$134	$ 8,641	$ 6,427	$ 9,095	$ 6,766
2	231	172	11,109	8,264	12,326	9,330
3	283	210	13,578	10,100	15,556	11,895
4	334	249	16,047	11,937	18,786	14,459
per avg. unit	258	192	12,329	9,200		
per room	51	38				
D. CONSTR.-REHAB. COSTS (+30%) BC1 = $2,132,520, BC3 = $1,300,000						
1	$191	$141	$ 9,155	$ 6,745	$ 9,637	$ 7,100
2	245	181	11,771	8,672	13,022	9,760
3	300	221	14,387	10,599	16,407	12,420
4	354	261	17,002	12,526	19,792	15,080
per avg. unit	273	201	13,105	9,654		
per room	54	40				

GRAPH A–2. CHANGE IN AVERAGE RENT VS. CHANGE IN CONSTRUCTION COST: NEW CONSTRUCTION AND REHABILITATION, NONPROFIT (BC1 AND BC3)

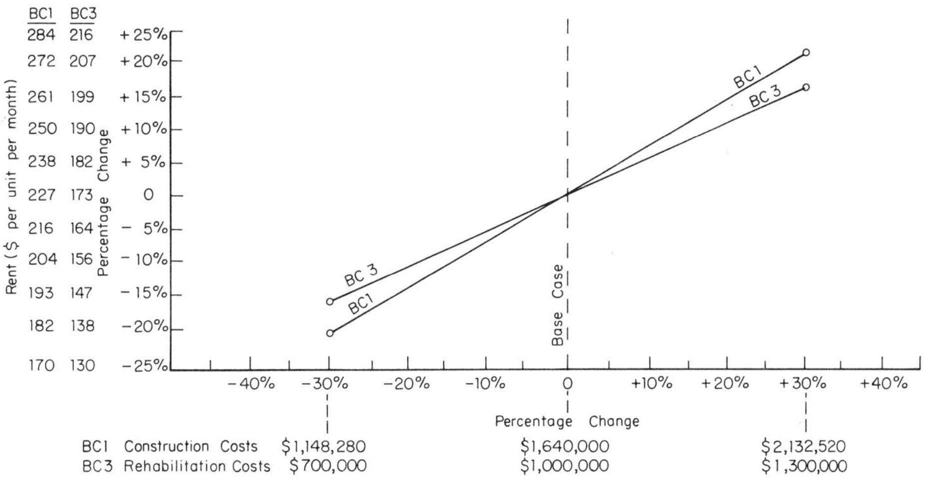

Changes in construction costs: Changes in rentals and income levels resulting from changes in construction costs are summarized below and presented in detail in Table A–7. Costs include only the costs of the construction or rehabilitation contract. Development fees, financing and carrying charges, and other development term expenses are excluded although these items may be affected indirectly. Graph A–2 plots the relationship between average unit rent and construction costs.

Percentage Change in Construction or Rehabilitation Costs	*Absolute Value of Construction or Rehabilitation Costs*		*Average Rent per Unit per Month*	
	BC1	BC3	BC1	BC3
–30%	$1,148,280	$ 700,000	$180	$144
BC 0	1,640,400	1,000,000	227	173
+10	1,804,440	1,100,000	242	182
+20	1,968,480	1,200,000	258	192
+30	2,132,520	1,300,000	273	201

GRAPH A–3. CHANGE IN AVERAGE RENT VS. CHANGE IN INTEREST RATE: NEW CONSTRUCTION AND REHABILITATION, NONPROFIT (BC1 AND BC3)

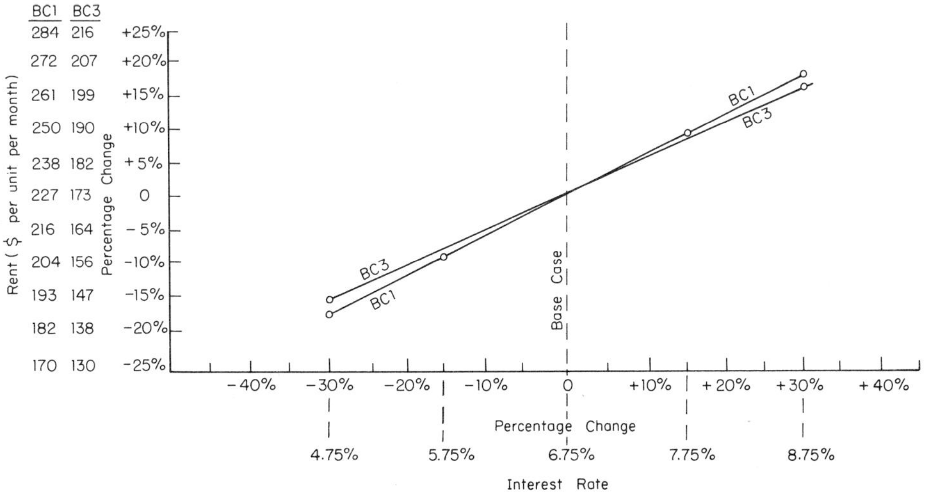

TABLE A–8. INTEREST RATES:
NEW CONSTRUCTION AND REHABILITATION, NONPROFIT (BC1 AND BC3)

Number of Bedrooms	*Market Rents (per month)*		*Minimum Income Levels (per year)*		*Maximum Income Levels (per year)*	
	BC1	BC3	BC1	BC3	BC1	BC3
A. INTEREST RATE = 4.75% (–30%)						
1	$131	$102	$ 6,305	$ 4,891	$ 6,637	$ 5,148
2	169	131	8,106	6,288	8,165	7,251
3	206	160	9,908	7,686	11,692	9,353
4	244	189	11,709	9,083	14,220	11,456
per avg. unit	188	146	9,025	7,001		
per room	38	29				
B. INTEREST RATE = 5.75% (–15%)						
1	$145	$111	$ 6,939	$ 5,329	$ 7,304	$ 5,609
2	186	143	8,921	6,852	10,002	7,844
3	227	174	10,903	8,374	12,741	10,078
4	268	206	12,886	9,897	15,459	12,312
per avg. unit	207	159	9,932	7,628		
per room	41	32				
C. INTEREST RATE = 7.75% (+15%)						
1	$173	$131	$ 8,307	$ 6,275	$ 8,745	$ 6,605
2	223	168	10,681	8,068	11,875	9,124
3	272	205	13,055	9,861	15,005	11,643
4	321	243	15,428	11,654	18,135	14,162
per avg. unit	248	187	11,891	8,983		
per room	49	37				
D. INTEREST RATE = 8.75% (+30%)						
1	$188	$141	$ 9,034	$ 6,778	$ 9,510	$ 7,134
2	242	182	11,616	8,714	12,859	9,804
3	296	222	14,197	10,651	16,207	12,474
4	350	262	16,778	12,587	19,556	15,144
per avg. unit	269	202	12,932	9,702		
per room	54	40				

Changes in interest rates: Changes in rentals and income levels resulting from interest rate changes are summarized below and presented in detail in Table A–8. Interest rate changes affect the amount charged on both the construction or rehabilitation loan and the mortgage loan. A yearly level annuity payment schedule is determined to calculate the annual debt service requirements for the assumed mortgage. Graph A–3 plots the relationship between average unit rent and the effective interest rate. The results indicate, for example, that the recent interest rate increase for mortgages insured by the Federal Housing Administration and the Veterans Administration from 6.75% to 7.50% will increase the average BC1 rent by 6.7%, from $227 to $242 per month, and average BC3 rent 6.4%, from $173 to $184.

Percentage Change in Interest Rate	*Absolute Value of Interest Rate*	*Average Rent per Unit per Month*	
		BC1	BC3
–30%	4.75%	$188	$146
–15	5.75	207	159
BC 0	6.75	227	173
+15	7.75	248	187
+30	8.75	269	202

TABLE A-9. MORTGAGE TERMS: NEW CONSTRUCTION AND REHABILITATION, NONPROFIT (BC1 AND BC3)

Number of Bedrooms	*Market Rents (per month)*		*Minimum Income Levels (per year)*		*Maximum Income Levels (per year)*	
	BC1	BC3	BC1	BC3	BC1	BC3
A. MORTGAGE TERM = 25 years (−37.5%)						
1	$176	$133	$ 8,444	$ 6,370	$ 8,889	$ 6,706
2	226	171	10,857	8,191	12,060	9,253
3	276	209	13,269	10,011	15,231	11,801
4	327	246	15,682	11,831	18,402	14,348
per avg. unit	252	190	12,087	9,119		
per room	50	38				
B. MORTGAGE TERM = 30 years (−25%)						
1	$168	$127	$ 8,042	$ 6,092	$ 8,465	$ 6,412
2	215	163	10,339	7,832	11,515	8,876
3	263	199	12,637	9,573	14,565	11,340
4	311	236	14,934	11,313	17,615	13,804
per avg. unit	240	182	11,511	8,720		
per room	48	36				
C. MORTGAGE TERM = 50 years (+25%)						
1	$154	$118	$ 7,406	$ 5,652	$ 7,795	$ 5,949
2	198	151	9,522	7,267	10,654	8,281
3	242	185	11,638	8,881	13,513	10,612
4	287	219	13,753	10,496	16,372	12,943
per avg. unit	221	169	10,601	8,090		
per room	44	34				

Mortgage term changes: Changes in rental and income level resulting from the mortgage term changes are summarized below and given in detail in Table A-9. For each mortgage term assumption, a level annuity payment schedule is determined in order to calculate annual debt service requirements. The relationship between average unit rent and mortgage term is plotted in Graphs A-4 and A-5. The dotted line represents the inverse relationship between average rent and mortgage term, since a term increase actually decreases rent, and vice versa.

Percentage Change in Mortgage Term	*Absolute Years of Mortgage Term*	*Average Rent per Unit per Month*	
		BC1	BC3
−37.5%	25	$252	$190
−25	30	240	182
BC 0	40	227	173
+25	50	221	169

GRAPH A–4. CHANGE IN AVERAGE RENT VS. CHANGE IN MORTGAGE TERM: NEW CONSTRUCTION, NONPROFIT (BC1)

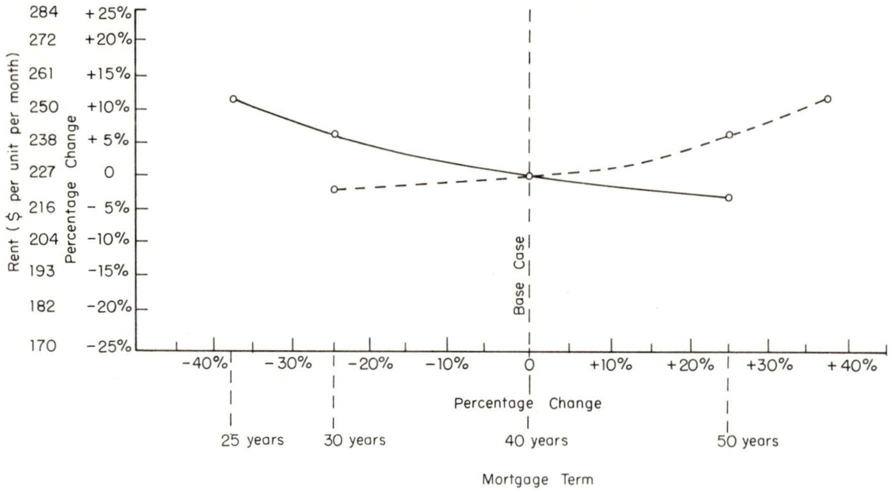

GRAPH A–5. CHANGE IN AVERAGE RENT VS. CHANGE IN MORTGAGE TERM: REHABILITATION, NONPROFIT (BC3)

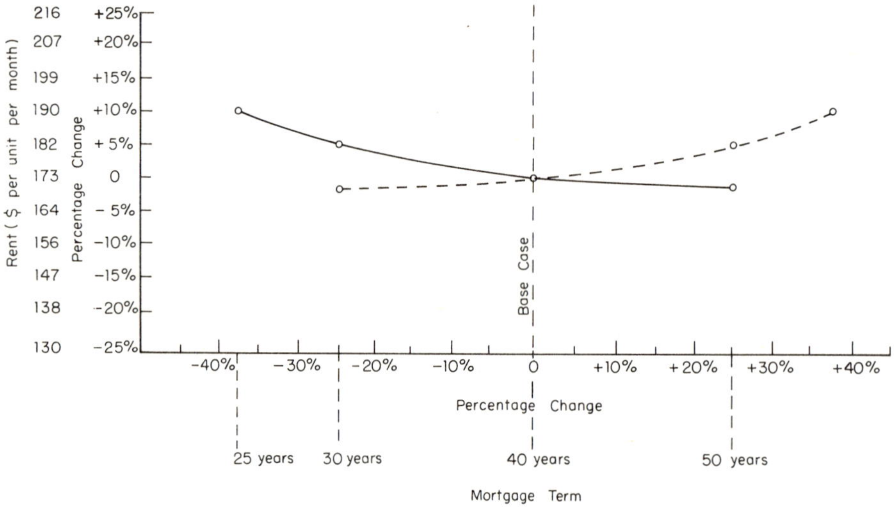

Operating expense changes: Changes in rentals and income levels resulting from operating expense changes are summarized below and given in detail in Table A–10. The relationship between average unit rent and operating expenses is plotted in Graph A–6.

Percentage Change in Operating Expenses	*Absolute Value of Operating Expenses*	*Average Rent per Unit per Month*	
		BC1	BC3
−30%	$35,070	$212	$157
−10	45,090	222	168
BC 0	50,100	227	173
+10	55,110	232	178
+30	65,130	242	188

TABLE A–10. OPERATING EXPENSES:
NEW CONSTRUCTION AND REHABILITATION, NONPROFIT (BC1 AND BC3)

Number of Bedrooms	*Market Rents (per month)*		*Minimum Income Levels (per year)*		*Maximum Income Levels (per year)*	
	BC1	BC3	BC1	BC3	BC1	BC3
A. OPERATING EXPENSES = $35,070 (–30%)						
1	$148	$110	$ 7,094	$ 5,278	$ 7,468	$ 5,556
2	190	141	9,121	6,786	10,233	7,775
3	232	173	11,148	8,294	12,998	9,994
4	274	204	13,175	9,802	15,763	12,213
per avg. unit	212	157	10,155	7,555		
per room	42	31				
B. OPERATING EXPENSES = $45,090 (–10%)						
1	$155	$117	$ 7,436	$ 5,620	$ 7,828	$ 5,916
2	199	151	9,561	7,226	10,696	8,238
3	243	184	11,686	8,832	13,564	10,560
4	288	217	13,810	10,438	16,432	12,882
per avg. unit	222	168	10,645	8,045		
per room	44	33				
C. OPERATING EXPENSES = $55,110 (+10%)						
1	$162	$124	$ 7,779	$ 5,963	$ 8,188	$ 6,276
2	208	160	10,001	7,666	11,159	8,701
3	255	195	12,223	9,370	14,130	11,126
4	301	231	14,446	11,073	17,101	13,551
per avg. unit	232	178	11,134	8,535		
per room	46	35				
D. OPERATING EXPENSES = $65,130 (+30%)						
1	$169	$131	$ 8,121	$ 6,305	$ 8,548	$ 6,637
2	218	169	10,441	8,106	11,662	9,164
3	266	206	12,761	9,907	14,696	11,692
4	314	244	15,082	11,709	17,770	14,220
per avg. unit	242	188	11,624	9,025		
per room	48	38				

GRAPH A–6. CHANGE IN AVERAGE RENT VS. CHANGE IN OPERATING EXPENSES: NEW CONSTRUCTION AND REHABILITATION, NONPROFIT (BC1 AND BC3)

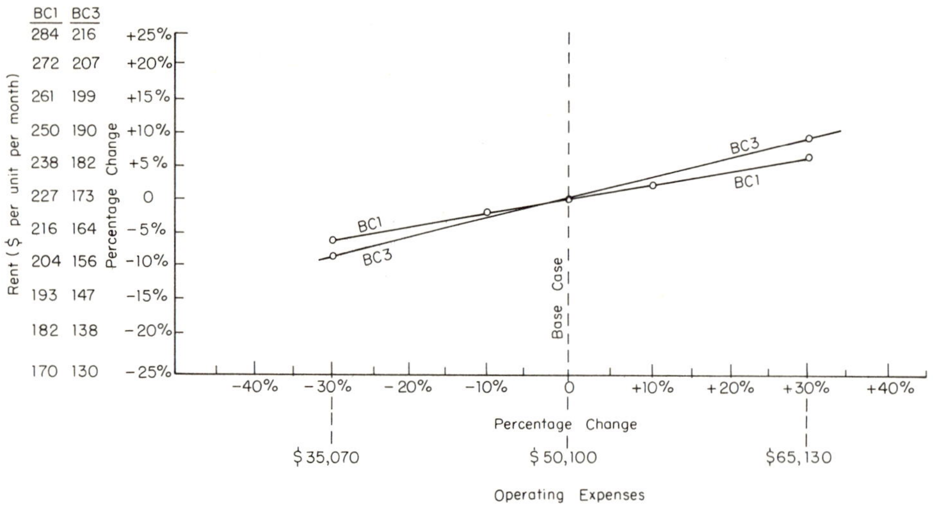

Changes in percentage of family income spent on rent: Changes in minimum and maximum income levels resulting from changes in the percentage of family income spent for rent are summarized below and presented in detail in Table A–11. If the percentage used in calculating income eligibility limits is changed, the population sector served will change accordingly. As the percentage factor increases, minimum and maximum income levels based on a given rent decrease, and vice versa. However, the BC's average unit rents remain unchanged since this factor only affects the proportion of family income considered equitable to spend for housing. (No graph is plotted for these variations because the relationship between average unit rent and the percentage of income spent on rent is constant.)

Percentage of Income Spent on Rent	*Average Rent per Unit per Month*		*Minimum Income Level Required*	
	BC1	BC3	BC1	BC3
15%	$227	$173	$18,149	$13,817
20	227	173	13,612	10,363
25	227	173	10,890	8,290
30	227	173	9,175	6,908
35	227	173	7,778	5,921

TABLE A–11. PERCENTAGE OF FAMILY INCOME SPENT FOR RENT: NEW CONSTRUCTION AND REHABILITATION, NONPROFIT (BC1 AND BC3)

Number of Bedrooms	*Market Rents (per month)*		*Minimum Income Levels (per year)*		*Maximum Income Levels (per year)*	
	BC1	BC3	BC1	BC3	BC1	BC3
A. PERCENTAGE OF INCOME SPENT FOR RENT = 15%						
1	$158	$121	$12,679	$ 9,652	$13,346	$10,160
2	204	155	16,302	12,410	17,791	13,695
3	249	190	19,924	15,168	22,236	17,229
4	294	224	23,547	17,926	26,681	20,764
per avg. unit	227	173	18,149	13,817		
per room	45	34				
B. PERCENTAGE OF INCOME SPENT FOR RENT = 20%						
1	$158	$121	$ 9,509	$ 7,239	$10,010	$ 7,620
2	204	155	12,226	9,308	13,501	10,429
3	249	190	14,943	11,376	16,993	13,238
4	294	224	17,660	13,444	20,484	16,047
per avg. unit	227	173	13,612	10,363		
per room	45	34				
C. PERCENTAGE OF INCOME SPENT FOR RENT = 30%						
1	$158	$121	$ 6,340	$ 4,826	$ 6,673	$ 5,080
2	204	155	8,151	6,205	9,211	7,163
3	249	190	9,962	7,584	11,750	9,246
4	294	224	11,773	8,963	14,288	11,329
per avg. unit	227	173	9,075	6,908		
per room	45	34				
D. PERCENTAGE OF INCOME SPENT FOR RENT = 35%						
1	$158	$121	$ 5,434	$ 4,137	$ 5,720	$ 4,354
2	204	155	6,986	5,319	7,986	6,230
3	249	190	8,539	6,501	10,252	8,106
4	294	224	10,092	7,682	12,517	9,982
per avg. unit	227	173	7,778	5,921		
per room	45	34				

TABLE A–12. REAL ESTATE TAXES (GROSS-SHELTER-RENT METHOD): NEW CONSTRUCTION AND REHABILITATION, NONPROFIT (BC1 AND BC3)

Number of Bedrooms	*Market Rents (per month)*		*Minimum Income Levels (per year)*		*Maximum Income Levels (per year)*	
	BC1	BC3	BC1	BC3	BC1	BC3
1	$157	$119	$ 7,519	$ 5,703	$ 7,915	$ 6,003
2	201	153	9,667	7,332	10,807	8,350
3	246	187	11,815	8,961	13,700	10,696
4	291	221	13,963	10,591	16,593	13,043

Changes in real estate taxes: Table A–12 shows changes in rentals and income levels resulting from changes in real estate taxes. The change is due to substituting the gross-shelter-rent method for the project-income method of computing real estate taxes. Gross-shelter-rent is defined as total project income less vacancy and contingency loss and all utility charges. Real estate taxes equal the assumed tax rate of 10% times the gross-shelter-rent. This change in assessment method for real estate taxes reduced average unit rent from $227 to $224 per month for BC1 and from $173 to $170 for BC3.

SECTION 236 PROGRAM

Steps 5 and 6: Section 236 Program Applied to Nonprofit Base Cases

Steps 5 and 6 determine the impact of Section 236 subsidies applied to the BC1 and BC3 projects. Basic rents and minimum income levels resulting under the subsidy formula are computed by HAM and compared with BC market rents and minimum incomes. Projections are made also of the units possible with various annual appropriations for the Section 236 Program.

Procedure: The Section 236 subsidy formula is applied to BC1 and BC3 as established in Steps 1 and 3. The assumptions underlying these calculations are:

- All project units are eligible to receive the maximum subsidy. Initial mortgage amount for the BC1 project is $2,215,610, and required market rents are $272,026 per year; corresponding BC3 amounts are $1,528,243 and $206,680.
- Section 236 periodic payments equal the difference between the debt service factor for the 6.75% market interest rate mortgage over a 40-year term, plus a 0.5% insurance premium on the declining balance, and the debt service factor for a 1% interest rate mortgage over a 40-year term. This payment is $47.201 per $1,000 of mortgage for the first year.
- Periodic payments in years 2 through 40 will continue to subsidize rents by an equivalent amount (although the payments' absolute value will gradually be reduced due to the decrease in the insurance premium charges).

Results: Table A-13 presents basic rents and minimum income levels resulting under the Section 236 Program applied to the BC1 and the BC3 projects. For comparison, the table also shows market rents required for these BCs without such subsidies. Subsidized rental charges for BC1 are 61.6% of unsubsidized rents, or a reduction in average unit rent from $227 to $140 per month. Average minimum income level is likewise reduced by 38.4%, from $10,900 to $6,700 per year. Corresponding BC3

TABLE A–13. SECTION 236 BASIC RENTS AND INCOME LEVELS: NEW CONSTRUCTION AND REHABILITATION, NONPROFIT (BC1 AND BC3)

Number of Bedrooms	*Market Rents (per month)*		*Section 236 Basic Rents (per month)*		*Minimum Income Levels (per year)*	
	BC1	BC3	BC1	BC3	BC1	BC3
1	$158	$121	$ 97	$ 79	$4,673	$3,783
2	204	155	126	101	6,033	4,846
3	249	190	153	124	7,364	5,941
4	294	224	181	146	8,694	7,004

GRAPH A–7. ANNUAL SECTION 236 APPROPRIATIONS VS. NUMBER OF UNITS PROVIDED: NEW CONSTRUCTION AND REHABILITATION, NONPROFIT (BC1 AND BC3)

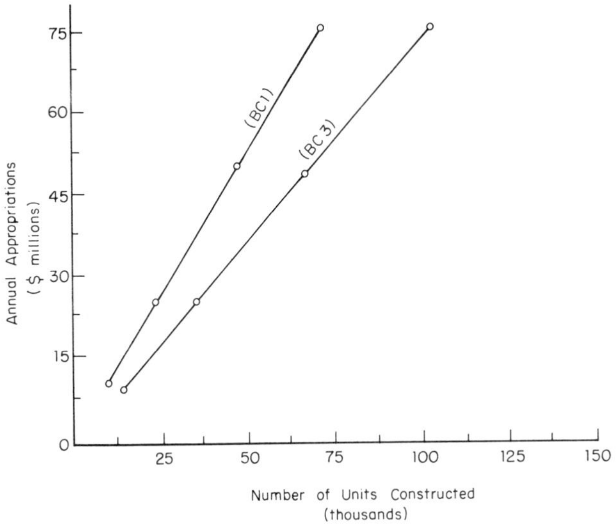

GRAPH A–8. ANNUAL SECTION 236 APPROPRIATIONS VS. NUMBER OF UNITS PROVIDED: NEW CONSTRUCTION, REHABILITATION, AND MIXED*, NONPROFIT (BC1 AND BC3)

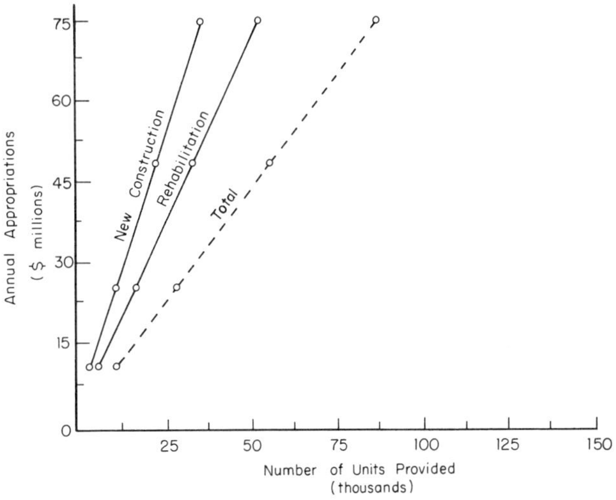

* One-half of the appropriation is used to subsidize new construction and one-half for rehabilitation.

figures are 65.1%, average rent reduction from $173 to $113, and income level reduction of 34.9% from $8,300 to $5,400.

The number of units possible with various annual appropriations for the Section 236 Program is determined by dividing the maximum allowable annual periodic payment for a new unit into the assumed annual appropriations. (Appropriation assumptions used are based on first year amounts established by HUDA 68. These appropriations are commitments to subsidize housing as required for the mortgage life at the annual levels indicated and should not be considered as expenditures in the year of appropriation only.) Results of these calculations are presented below and in Graph A–7.

Annual Section 236 Appropriations	*Number of Units Provided*	
	BC1	BC3
$10,000,000	9,589	13,857
25,000,000	23,973	34,642
50,000,000	47,946	69,285
75,000,000	71,918	103,927

Step 7: Section 236 Program Applied to a Nonprofit Base Cases Mix

This step determines the impact of Section 236 subsidies if one-half the annual appropriation is used to subsidize BC1 projects and one-half BC3 projects. This step's procedure duplicates the assumptions of Steps 5 and 6 for the new construction and rehabilitation BCs, respectively. Both subsidized and unsubsidized rents and income levels are the same as those calculated separately for new construction and rehabilitation (see Table A–13). The results of this mix in terms of units possible with various annual appropriations for the Section 236 Program are presented below and in Graph A–8. The units provided by both the new construction and rehabilitation portions of these appropriations are shown separately in this graph as well as the combined total.

Annual Section 236 Appropriations	*Number of Units Provided*		
	Total	BC1	BC3
$10,000,000	11,723	4,795	6,928
25,000,000	29,307	11,986	17,321
50,000,000	58,615	23,973	34,642
75,000,000	87,922	35,959	51,963

Steps 8 and 9: Section 236 Program Applied to Limited-Dividend Base Cases

These steps determine the impact of Section 236 subsidies applied to BC2 and BC4 projects. The subsidy formula is the same as that outlined in Step 5. Basic rents and minimum income levels resulting

TABLE A–14. SECTION 236 BASIC RENTS AND INCOME LEVELS: NEW CONSTRUCTION AND REHABILITATION, LIMITED-DIVIDEND (BC2 AND BC4)

Number of Bedrooms	*Market Rents (per month)*		*Section 236 Basic Rents (per month)*		*Minimum Income Levels (per year)*	
	BC2	BC4	BC2	BC4	BC2	BC4
1	$156	$119	$101	$ 81	$4,829	$3,871
2	201	153	130	104	6,222	4,977
3	246	187	159	127	7,615	6,083
4	291	221	188	150	9,008	7,189

under this formula are computed by HAM and compared with BC market rents and minimum incomes. Projections are also made of the units possible with various annual appropriations for the Section 236 Program.

Procedure: The Section 236 subsidy formula is applied to the BCs established in Steps 1 and 3. The assumptions underlying these calculations are:

- All project units are eligible to receive the maximum subsidy. Initial mortgage amount for the BC2 project is $2,025,305, and required market rents are $268,772; for BC4 $1,398,165 and $204,507.
- Periodic payments are equal to $47.201 per $1,000 of mortgage for the first year.
- Periodic payments in years 2 through 40 will continue to subsidize rents by an equivalent amount.

Results: Table A–14 presents basic rents and minimum income levels resulting under the Section 236 Program applied to BC2 and BC4. Market rents required for the projects without such subsidies are also shown in the table for comparison. For BC2, subsidized rental charges are 64.5% of unsubsidized rents; for BC4, 67.8%. This means a rent reduction for an average BC2 unit from $224 to $145 per month; for BC4, from $170 to $115. The average minimum income level is likewise reduced for BC2, to 64.5% of the original levels, from $10,750 to $6,950 per year, and for BC4, 67.8%, from $8,200 to $5,550.

The units possible with various annual appropriations for the Section 236 Program are also determined by dividing the maximum allowable periodic payment each year for a unit into the assumed annual appropriation. Results of these calculations are presented below and in Graph A–9.

Annual Section 236 Appropriations	*Number of Units Provided*	
	BC2	BC4
$10,000,000	10,500	15,210
25,000,000	26,250	38,000
50,000,000	52,500	76,000
75,000,000	78,750	114,000

GRAPH A–9. ANNUAL SECTION 236 APPROPRIATIONS VS. NUMBER OF UNITS PROVIDED: NEW CONSTRUCTION AND REHABILITATION, LIMITED-DIVIDEND (BC2 AND BC4)

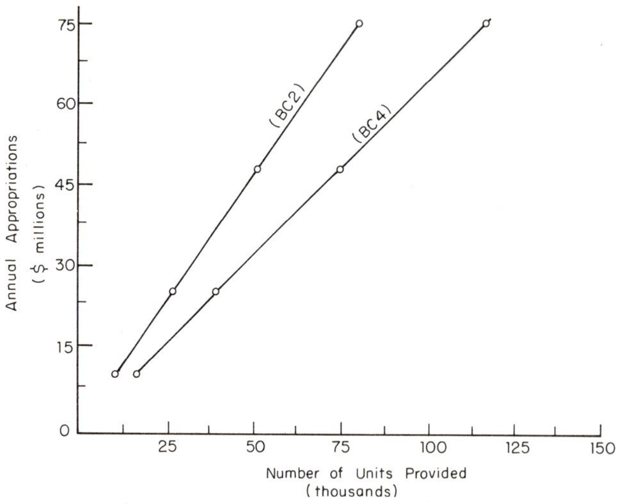

Step 10: Section 236 Program Applied to New Construction and Rehabilitation Base Cases with a Mix of Sponsorship

This step determines the impact of Section 236 subsidies if one-half the annual appropriation subsidizes nonprofit sponsored projects and one-half limited-dividend sponsored projects. This assumption is applied to new construction and rehabilitation BCs independently.

The procedure for a mixed-sponsorship new construction project duplicates that of Steps 5 and 8 for BC1 and BC2 respectively. Both subsidized and unsubsidized rents and income levels in this mixed housing equal those calculated separately for the two types of projects (see Tables A–15 and A–16). Results for new construction with a mix of sponsorship in terms of units possible with various annual appropriations for the Section 236 Program are presented below and in Graph A–10.

Annual Section 236 Appropriations	*Number of New Construction Units Provided*		
	Total	BC1	BC2
$10,000,000	10,025	4,800	5,225
25,000,000	25,100	12,000	13,100
50,000,000	50,250	24,000	26,250
75,000,000	75,350	35,950	39,400

The procedure for a mixed-sponsorship rehabilitation project duplicates that of Steps 6 and 9 for BC3 and BC4, respectively. Both subsidized and unsubsidized rents and income levels in mixed-sponsorship housing are the same as those calculated separately for the two types of projects (see Tables A–17 and A–18). Results of the mixed-sponsorship rehabilitation in terms of the units possible with various appropriations for the Section 236 Program are presented below and in Graph A–11.

Annual Section 236 Appropriations	*Number of Rehabilitation Units Provided*		
	Total	BC3	BC4
$10,000,000	14,500	6,900	7,600
25,000,000	36,300	17,300	19,000
50,000,000	72,650	34,650	38,000
75,000,000	108,950	51,950	57,000

GRAPH A–10. ANNUAL SECTION 236 APPROPRIATIONS VS. NUMBER OF UNITS PROVIDED: NEW CONSTRUCTION, MIXED SPONSORSHIP * (BC1 AND BC2)

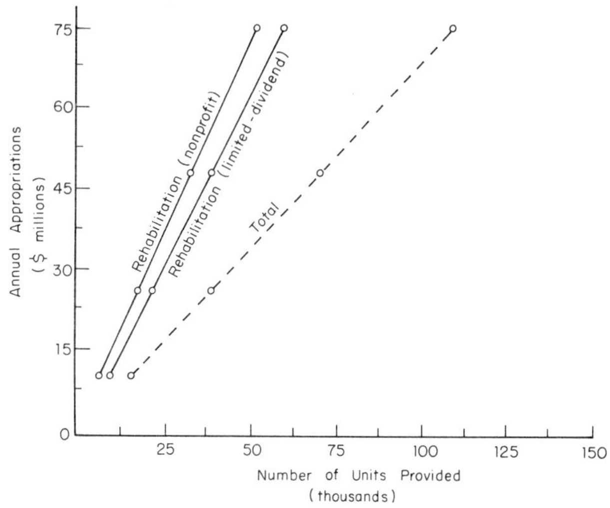

GRAPH A–11. ANNUAL SECTION 236 APPROPRIATIONS VS. NUMBER OF UNITS PROVIDED: REHABILITATION, MIXED SPONSORSHIP * (BC3 AND BC4)

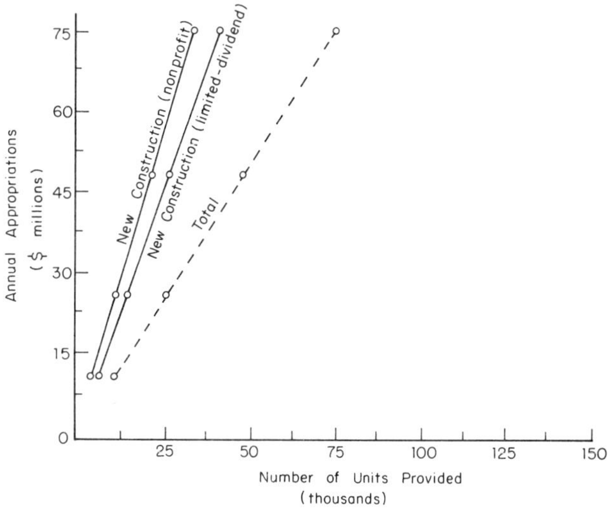

* One-half of the appropriation is used to subsidize new construction under nonprofit sponsorship and one-half for new construction under limited-dividend sponsorship. The number of units provided by the respective portions of the appropriations are shown separately in this graph as well as the combined total number.

TABLE A–15. SECTION 236 UNIT DISTRIBUTION: NEW CONSTRUCTION AND REHABILITATION, NONPROFIT (BC1 AND BC3)

Number of Bedrooms	*Market Rents*		*Sec. 236 Rents*		*Minimum Income Levels*	
	BC1	BC3	BC1	BC3	BC1	BC3
A. MIX #1						
0	$119	$ 93	$ 73	$ 60	$3,490	$2,859
1	166	130	102	83	4,886	4,002
2	214	167	131	107	6,282	5,145
3	262	204	160	131	7,679	6,289
B. MIX #2						
2	$201	$152	$124	$ 99	$5,958	$4,774
3	245	186	152	122	7,282	5,835
4	290	219	179	144	8,607	6,896
5	334	253	207	166	9,931	7,957

TABLE A–16. SECTION 236 OPERATING EXPENSES: NEW CONSTRUCTION AND REHABILITATION, NONPROFIT (BC1 AND BC3)

Number of Bedrooms	*Market Rents*		*Sec. 236 Rents*		*Minimum Income Levels*	
	BC1	BC3	BC1	BC3	BC1	BC3
A. EXPENSES *decrease* 30%						
1	$148	$110	$ 87	$ 68	$4,180	$3,261
2	190	141	112	87	5,374	4,193
3	232	173	137	107	6,569	5,125
4	274	204	162	126	7,763	6,057
B. EXPENSES *increase* 30%						
1	$169	$131	$108	$ 89	$5,207	$4,288
2	218	169	139	115	6,694	5,513
3	266	206	170	140	8,182	6,738
4	314	244	201	166	9,669	7,964

TABLE A–17. SECTION 236 INTEREST RATE CHANGES: NEW CONSTRUCTION AND REHABILITATION, NONPROFIT (BC1 AND BC3)

Number of Bedrooms	*Market Rents*		*Sec. 236 Rents*		*Minimum Income Levels*	
	BC1	BC3	BC1	BC3	BC1	BC3
A. RATE of 5.75%						
1	$145	$111	$ 95	$ 76	$4,539	$3,668
2	186	143	122	98	5,836	4,716
3	227	174	149	120	7,133	5,765
4	268	206	176	142	8,430	6,813
B. RATE OF 7.75%						
1	$173	$131	$100	$ 80	$4,808	$3,854
2	223	168	129	103	6,182	4,955
3	272	205	157	126	7,555	6,056
4	321	243	186	149	8,929	7,157

TABLE A–18. PERCENTAGE OF INCOME SPENT FOR SECTION 236 RENT: NEW CONSTRUCTION AND REHABILITATION, NONPROFIT (BC1 AND BC3)

Number of Bedrooms	*Market Rents*		*Sec. 236 Rents*		*Minimum Income Levels*	
	BC1	BC3	BC1	BC3	BC1	BC3
A. INCOME FACTOR 15%						
1	$158	$121	$ 98	$ 79	$ 7,822	$ 5,291
2	204	155	126	101	10,057	8,089
3	249	190	154	124	12,292	9,886
4	294	224	182	146	14,527	11,684
B. INCOME FACTOR 35%						
1	$158	$121	$ 98	$ 79	$ 3,352	$ 2,696
2	204	155	126	101	4,310	3,467
3	249	190	154	124	5,268	4,237
4	294	224	182	146	6,226	5,007

Steps 11 and 12: Variable Testing for Section 236 Program Applied to Nonprofit Base Cases

These steps determine the impact of Section 236 subsidies applied to BC1 and BC3 projects with changes in certain BC cost category assumptions. Reference is also made to the rents and incomes per average unit developed in Step 5 for the Section 236 Program applied to a BC1 project with the original BC assumptions, and likewise to Step 6 for a similar BC3 project. Comparative projections are included of the number of new and rehabilitated housing units possible with various annual appropriations for the Section 236 Program, given the cost changes. These projections are calculated by dividing the maximum allowable periodic payment each year (equal to the market rent less the subsidized basic rent each year) into the assumed annual appropriations.

The impact of these systematic cost changes on both new and rehabilitated units provided and rents and incomes required follow.

Construction and rehabilitation cost changes: Table A–19 presents basic rents and minimum income levels resulting under the subsidy formula as construction and rehabilitation costs vary. Resulting market rents are included for comparison. Average market and Section 236 basic rents for the various conditions follow.

TABLE A–19. SECTION 236 CONSTRUCTION AND REHABILITATION COSTS: NEW CONSTRUCTION AND REHABILITATION, NONPROFIT (BC1 AND BC3)

Number of Bedrooms	*Market Rents*		*Sec. 236 Rents*		*Minimum Income Levels*	
	BC1	BC3	BC1	BC3	BC1	BC3
A. COSTS DECREASED 30%						
1	$126	$101	$ 81	$ 69	$ 3,905	$ 3,290
2	162	129	105	88	5,021	4,230
3	198	158	128	108	6,137	5,170
4	234	187	151	127	7,253	6,110
B. COSTS INCREASED 30%						
1	$191	$141	$114	$ 89	$ 5,476	$ 4,257
2	245	181	147	114	7,041	5,473
3	300	221	179	139	8,605	6,689
4	354	261	212	165	10,170	7,906

Percentage Change in Construction-Rehabilitation Costs	*Average Market Rent*		*Average Section 236 Rent*	
	BC1	BC3	BC1	BC3
−30%	$180	$144	$116	$ 98
BC 0	227	173	140	113
+30	273	201	163	127

Total units possible under these variations with different annual appropriations for the Program follow.

Annual Section 236 Appropriation	*New and Rehabilitated Units Provided*					
			Costs −30%		*Costs +30%*	
	BC1	BC3	BC1	BC3	BC1	BC3
$10,000,000	9,589	13,857	13,020	18,110	7,595	11,233
25,000,000	23,973	34,642	35,590	45,270	18,988	28,082
50,000,000	47,976	69,285	65,180	90,540	37,975	56,165
75,000,000	71,918	103,927	97,770	135,810	56,962	84,248

Procedure for unit distribution changes: The BCs assume a unit size distribution which indirectly affects calculation of development costs, occupancy expenses, and rents and incomes. To test these effects, two unit distribution changes were made:

Type of Bedroom Unit	BC *Bedroom Mix*	*Mix #1*	*Mix #2*
efficiency	—	38	—
1 bedroom	12	38	—
2 bedroom	38	12	12
3 bedroom	38	12	12
4 bedroom	12	—	38
5 bedroom or more	—	—	38

Mix #1 provides more small units, requiring certain changes in BC assumptions, presented in the calculations below.

- Total construction and rehabilitation costs decline from $1,640,400 to $1,172,600, and from $1,000,000 to $720,120, respectively; breakdown by unit size follows:

Construction:			
38 efficiency	(2.5 rm) units	@ $ 8,550 per unit	= $324,900
38 one bedrm.	(3.5 rm) units	@ 11,950 per unit	= 454,100
12 two bedrm.	(4.5 rm) units	@ 14,900 per unit	= 178,800
12 three bedrm.	(5.5 rm) units	@ 17,900 per unit	= 214,800
Rehabilitation:			
38 efficiency	(2.5 rm) units	@ $ 5,240 per unit	= $199,120
38 one bedrm.	(3.5 rm) units	@ 7,300 per unit	= 277,400
12 two bedrm.	(4.5 rm) units	@ 9,400 per unit	= 112,800
12 three bedrm.	(5.5 rm) units	@ 10,900 per unit	= 130,800

- Loans, based on 70% of construction and 75% of rehabilitation costs, decline respectively from $1,110,000 to $820,820, and from $750,000 to $540,000.

- Total operating expenses, estimated at $100/room/annum, decline from $50,100 to $34,800 as the room count declines from 501 to 348 respectively.

Mix #2 provides more large units, requiring certain changes in the BC assumptions outlined in the calculations below:

- Total construction and rehabilitation costs increase, respectively, from $1,640,400 to $2,134,000, and from $1,000,000 to $1,322,800; breakdown by unit size follows:

Construction:				
12 two bedrm.	(4.5 rm) units	@ $14,900	per unit =	$178,800
12 three bedrm.	(5.5 rm) units	@ 17,900	per unit =	214,800
38 four bedrm.	(6.5 rm) units	@ 20,900	per unit =	794,200
38 five bedrm.	(7.5 rm) units	@ 24,900	per unit =	946,200
Rehabilitation:				
12 two bedrm.	(4.5 rm) units	@ $ 9,400	per unit =	$112,800
12 three bedrm.	(5.5 rm) units	@ 10,900	per unit =	130,800
38 four bedrm.	(6.5 rm) units	@ 12,750	per unit =	484,500
38 five bedrm.	(7.5 rm) units	@ 15,600	per unit =	594,700

- Loans, based on 70% of construction and 75% of rehabilitation costs, increase respectively from $1,110,000 to $1,493,800, and from $750,000 to $922,100.
- Total operating expenses, estimated at $100/room/annum, increase from $50,100 to $65,200, with room count increasing from 501 to 652.

Unit distribution changes: Table A–15 shows basic rents and minimum income levels resulting under the subsidy formula with changes in unit distribution. For comparison this table also shows resultant market rents. Average market and Section 236 basic rents for the several conditions follow.

	Average Market Rent		*Average Section 236 Rent*	
Unit Distribution	BC1	BC3	BC1	BC3
Mix #1	$165	$129	$101	$ 83
BC Mix	227	173	140	113
Mix #2	291	220	180	144

New units possible with these distributions under various annual appropriations for the Program follow.

Annual Section 236 Appropriations	*Number of Units Provided*					
	BC Mix		*Mix #1*		*Mix #2*	
	BC1	BC3	BC1	BC3	BC1	BC3
$10,000,000	9,589	13,857	12,950	17,970	7,520	10,990
25,000,000	23,973	34,642	32,400	44,930	18,790	27,440
50,000,000	47,946	69,285	64,800	89,850	37,580	58,870
75,000,000	71,918	103,927	97,200	134,780	56,780	82,310

Interest rate changes: Table A–18 shows basic rents and minimum income levels resulting under the subsidy formula with changing interest rates; these calculations require determination of the periodic subsidy payments for each rate. The periodic payments equal the debt service factor for the effective market rate, assuming level annuity interest and amortization for a 40-year term and a 0.5% mortgage insurance premium on the declining balance, less the debt service factor for a 1% mortgage over a 40-year term. Average market and Section 236 basic rents for different interest rates follow:

Effective Interest Rate	*Average Market Rent*		*Average Section 236 Rent*	
	BC1	BC3	BC1	BC3
5.75%	$207	$159	$135	$109
BC 6.75%	227	173	140	113
7.75%	248	187	143	115

New units possible with these changes under various annual appropriations follow.

Section 236 Appropriations	*Numbers of New and Rehabilitated Units Provided*					
	BC Rate		*5.75% rate*		*7.75% rate*	
	BC1	BC3	BC1	BC3	BC1	BC3
$10,000,000	9,589	13,857	11,650	16,830	7,945	11,584
25,000,000	23,973	34,642	29,110	42,070	19,850	28,960
50,000,000	47,946	69,285	58,230	84,130	39,700	57,920
75,000,000	71,918	103,927	87,340	126,200	59,550	86,840

Operating expense changes: Table A–16 shows basic rents and minimum income levels resulting under the subsidy formula with changes in operating expenses. For comparison this table shows market rents resulting from these cost changes. Average market and Section 236 basic rents for the different operating expense levels follow.

Percentage Change in Operating Expense	*Average Market Rent*		*Average Section 236 Rent*	
	BC1	BC3	BC1	BC3
−30%	$212	$157	$125	$ 97
BC 0%	227	173	140	113
+30%	242	188	155	128

The units possible with these changed expense levels under various annual appropriations equal those of the BC condition. Thus the subsidy amount applied to the project is constant for all three conditions. The fact that operating expenses are not affected by the subsidy formula is an important limitation of the program.

Changes in percentage of family income spent for rent: Table A–18 shows minimum income levels resulting under the subsidy formula with changes in percentage of family income spent for rent. When the percentage factor used in calculating eligibility is decreased, the income sector served is scaled upwards, and vice versa. Basic rents do not change, because the percentage factor only affects the proportion of a family's income which is considered equitable to spend for housing. Since this analysis has assumed maximum subsidies for all units, a change in the percentage of family income spent for rent does not affect the number of units possible under various annual appropriations for the program.

Other Subsidy Programs

Step 13: Section 235 Program Applied to Special New Construction and Rehabilitation Base Cases

Step 13 determines the impact of Section 235 [1] subsidies applied to special new construction projects and special rehabilitation projects. Basic mortgage payment and minimum and maximum income levels resulting under the subsidy formula are computed by HAM and compared with market mortgage payments and income levels. Projections are also made of the new or rehabilitated units possible with various annual appropriations for the Section 235 home ownership program.

Procedure: The Section 235 subsidy formula is applied to special BCs for new construction and rehabilitation. New dwelling costs were derived from maximum mortgage amounts established by HUDA 68. Rehabilitated dwelling costs assume rehabilitation costs to be approximately 70% of new construction limits. Three typical projects are determined for both new construction and rehabilitation.

Project Type	*Dwelling Cost* BC1	*Dwelling Cost* BC3
1	$15,000 [2]	$10,000
2	17,500	12,500
3	20,000	15,000

For all projects it was assumed that 100% of dwelling cost is mortgaged and maximum subsidy applied. The market mortgage debt service factor is based on yearly level annuity payments for a 6.75% interest rate over a 30-year term, with a 0.5% mortgage insurance premium on the declining balance. The subsidized debt service factor includes payments for interest and principal at a 1% rate over 30 years. Minimum income levels based on this formula (rule #1) are calculated assuming 20% of the home owner's gross income spent on the mortgage obligations. Minimum levels based on the alternative formula (rule #2) assume 20% of gross income spent on the mortgage obligations and the required home insurance and real estate taxes; the latter two are estimated at 2% of dwelling cost. Maximum income levels are determined on the basis of 20% of adjusted income spent for the market mortgage principal, interest, insurance premiums, real estate taxes, and home insurance.

Results for new construction BCs: Basic mortgage payments and minimum income levels, for both subsidy rules, resulting under the Section 235 Program applied to the new construction BCs are shown in Table A–20. Market mortgage obligations for these projects are also shown for comparison. Subsidized mortgage payments are 46.6% of unsubsidized payments. Minimum incomes are likewise reduced to 46.6% of original levels applying subsidy rule #1. Subsidy rule #2, however, probably will be the more realistic eligibility requirement. This rule, resulting in a minimum income of $5,140 per year for a $17,500 unit, also takes into account required expenditures for real estate taxes and home insurance. Beyond this amount, the family must still cover, out of available income, other operating expenses, which could total as much again as mortgage obligations. Evidently the government is assuming that the differential between the 20% of income spent for rent, used here for calculating minimum incomes, and the normal 25% factor will cover these expenses. Even the minimum income calculated under rule #2 may not allow enough surplus for these additional expenses. In this event, the families served will require increased incomes approaching the maximum of $9,665 for the $17,500 unit. (See Table A–20.)

The units of new housing possible with various annual appropriations for Section 235 are determined by dividing the maximum allowable periodic payment for a new unit into the assumed annual appropriations. The periodic payment for the minimum income under either subsidy rule is the same; the differential in 20% of income is the slack used for other occupancy expenses. Results of these calculations are presented below and in Graph A–12.

[1] Section 235's provisions are detailed on p. 35.

[2] The mortgage principal for one unit cannot exceed $15,000. This limit is raised to $17,500 in geographical areas where cost levels require it. For a family of 5 or more persons, $17,500 is the basic limit and $20,000 the exception.

TABLE A–20. SECTION 235 BASIC RENTS AND INCOME LEVELS PER YEAR: NEW CONSTRUCTION AND REHABILITATION, NONPROFIT (BC1 AND BC3)

Dwelling Cost	*Market[1] Mortgage Payments*	*Section 235[2] Mortgage Payments*	*Minimum[3] Income Levels*	*Minimum[4] Income Levels*	*Maximum[5] Income Levels*
A. NEW CONSTRUCTION (BC1)					
$15,000	$1,254	$581	$2,905	$4,405	$ 8,370
17,500	1,463	678	3,390	5,140	9,665
20,000	1,671	775	3,875	5,875	10,355
B. REHABILITATION (BC3)					
$10,000	$ 836	$387	$1,935	$2,935	$ 5,790
12,500	1,045	484	2,420	3,670	7,075
15,000	1,254	581	2,905	4,405	8,370

[1] Based on 6.75%, 30-year mortgage, plus 0.5% mortgage premium.

[2] Based on 1%, 30-year mortgage.

[3] Based on 20% of gross family income paid for mortgage principal and interest.

[4] Based on 20% of gross family income paid for mortgage principal, interest, real estate taxes, and home insurance.

[5] Based on 20% of net family income paid for principal, interest, premiums, real estate taxes, and insurance. Net income is taken as gross income less $300 for each minor child. Calculations assume taxes and insurance equal to 2% of the dwelling cost and two children in each family.

If, as suggested above, the maximum subsidy is not applied in practice, these results will be adjusted upwards.

Annual Section 235 Appropriations	*Number of New Construction Units Provided*		
	$ 15,000	*$17,500*	*$20,000*
$10,000,000	14,724	12,716	11,155
25,000,000	36,810	31,790	27,887
50,000,000	73,620	63,580	55,775
75,000,000	110,430	95,370	83,662

Results for rehabilitation BCs: Basic mortgage payments and minimum income levels for both subsidy rules resulting under the Section 235 Program applied to nonprofit rehabilitation BCs are shown in Table A–20. Market mortgage obligations for these projects are also shown for comparison. Under rule #1, subsidized mortgage payments and minimum incomes are 45.9% of unsubsidized amounts. However, subsidy rule #2 will probably be effective in determining minimum income eligibility.

The number of rehabilitated units possible with various annual appropriations for the Section 235 Program, calculated in the same manner as the new construction units, follow, and are plotted in Graph A–12. Adjustments may have to be made if the full subsidy is not applied.

GRAPH A–12. ANNUAL SECTION 235 APPROPRIATIONS VS. NUMBER OF UNITS PROVIDED: NEW CONSTRUCTION AND REHABILITATION, NONPROFIT (BC1 AND BC3)

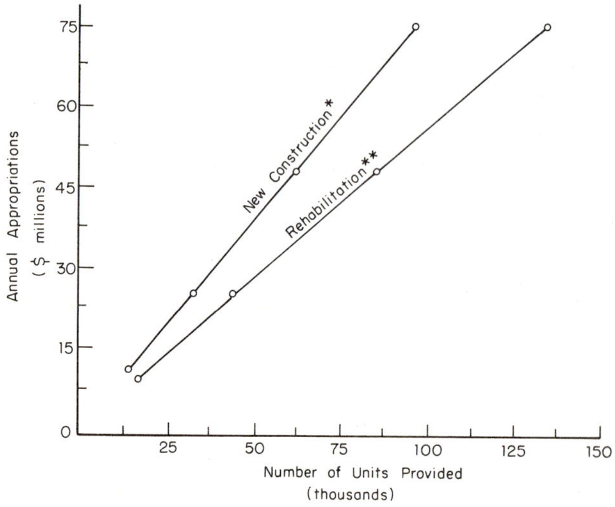

* Based on dwelling cost of $17,500.

** Based on dwelling cost of $12,500.

Annual Section 235 Appropriations	*Number of Rehabilitation Units Provided*		
	$ 10,000	*$ 12,500*	*$ 15,000*
$10,000,000	22,296	17,823	14,724
25,000,000	55,710	44,620	36,810
50,000,000	111,420	89,240	73,620
75,000,000	169,130	133,860	110,430

Step 14: Section 221(h) Program Applied to Nonprofit Rehabilitation Base Case

HUDA 68 amended Section 221(h) of the National Housing Act, reducing the program's effective interest rate from 3% to 1% and increasing the appropriation to $50 million, based on total outstanding mortgage principal. The program allows financing of up to 100% of the property's appraised value before rehabilitation plus the rehabilitation cost itself. The maximum mortgage amount is $15,000 per unit at a 1% below market interest rate with maturity determined by the FHA. (The effective interest rate may be raised to 3% if tenant incomes increase sufficiently.) This interest rate subsidy differs from the periodic payments applied under the Section 235 or 236 formulas, although the effect on rental charges is very similar. The difference is that under Section 221(h), the below-market-rate mortgage is granted by the government directly, rather than through private mortgages. The mortgage is then discounted by the FNMA in the secondary mortgage market, with subsidies attached out of general revenues to bring the 1% interest up to a market rate.

Step 14 determines the impact of Section 221(h) subsidies applied to a rehabilitation (nonprofit) project, assuming that the 6.75% market rate mortgage over a 40-year term is directly subsidized to an effective 1% rate. Table A-21 presents basic rents and minimum income levels resulting from this subsidy formula, computed by HAM and compared with BC market rents. Subsidized rental charges are 65.1% of unsubsidized rents, a reduction in average unit rent from $173 to $113 per month.

GRAPH A-13. ANNUAL SECTION 221(H) APPROPRIATIONS VS. NUMBER OF UNITS PROVIDED: REHABILITATION, NONPROFIT (BC3)

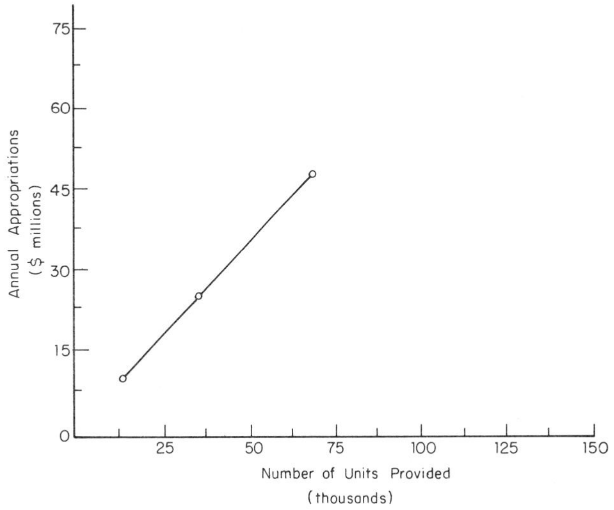

Average minimum incomes are likewise reduced to 65.1% of original levels, from $8,300 to $5,400 per year. These rents and incomes, both subsidized and unsubsidized, are the same as for the Section 236 Program applied to a rehabilitation project, given the particular BC assumptions. However, the Section 221(h) subsidy formula would prove less susceptible to fluctuations in effective interest rate if such variations were tested, because of the direct rather than the indirect interest rate reduction.

The number of rehabilitated units possible with various appropriations for Section 221(h) is determined by dividing the outstanding mortgage principal for a rehabilitated unit into the assumed appropriations. This method reflects the fact that the government actually writes the mortgage under Section 221(h). The units possible are greatly reduced in comparison with a projection based on dividing the maximum allowable interest rate subsidy each year into the appropriations. The latter method provides

TABLE A-21. SECTION 221(H) BASIC RENTS AND INCOME LEVELS: REHABILITATION, NONPROFIT (BC3)

Number of Bedrooms	*Market Rents (per month)*	*Section 221(h) Basic Rents (per month)*	*Minimum Income Levels (per month)*
1	$121	$ 79	$3,783
2	155	101	4,846
3	190	124	5,941
4	224	146	7,004

for the same number of units as under the Section 236 Program, at least in the first year. Results for both methods of calculation are presented below and in Graph A–13.

Maximum Section 221(h) Appropriations	*Number of Rehabilitated Units Provided*	
	Mortgage Basis	*Interest Basis*
$10,000,000	656	13,857
25,000,000	1,638	34,642
50,000,000	3,276	69,285

Step 15: Rent Supplement Program Applied to Nonprofit Base Cases

Although there are serious limitations in the program because of small appropriations and numerous restrictions as to types of projects to which supplements can be applied, rent supplements are effective in reducing rents, especially when combined with another subsidy program. Our examples, however, apply the supplements to the BCs independent of any combinations.

This step determines the impact of the Rent Supplement Program applied to a new construction (nonprofit) BC and to a rehabilitation (nonprofit) BC where all units in each project are eligible for maximum supplement payments at 70% of market rents. Table A–22 presents basic rents and minimum income levels resulting under this subsidy formula, calculated by HAM and compared with market rents for both project types. Subsidized rental charges are equal in each case to 30% of unsubsidized rents.

GRAPH A–14. ANNUAL RENT SUPPLEMENT APPROPRIATIONS VS. NUMBER OF UNITS PROVIDED: NEW CONSTRUCTION AND REHABILITATION, NONPROFIT (BC1 AND BC3)

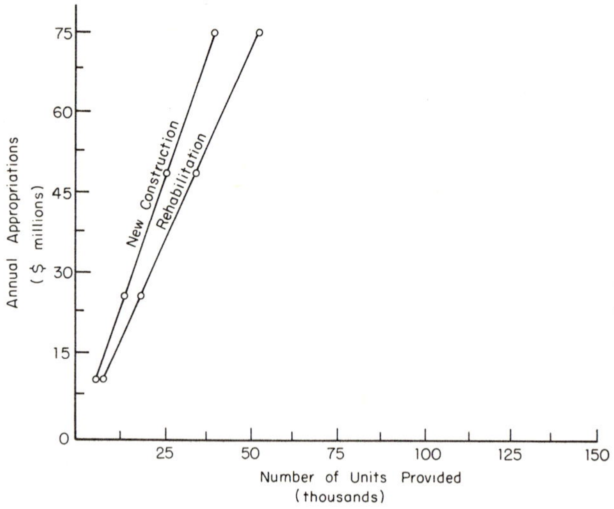

Minimum incomes are likewise reduced to 30% of original levels. For example, average market rents for the new construction project have been reduced from $227 to $68 per month. Corresponding average income levels are $10,900 and $3,250 respectively. Income limits for both new and rehabilitation projects for most local areas lie within the Section 101 Rent Supplement Income Limits established by the FHA for each area.

The number of new or rehabilitated housing units possible with various annual appropriations for the Rent Supplement Program is determined by dividing

TABLE A–22. RENT SUPPLEMENT BASIC RENTS AND INCOME LEVELS: NEW CONSTRUCTION AND REHABILITATION, NONPROFIT (BC1 AND BC3)

Number of Bedrooms	*Market Rents (per month)*	*Rent Supplement Basic Rents * (per month)*	*Minimum Income Levels (per year)*
A. NEW CONSTRUCTION (BC1)			
1	$158	$47	$2,260
2	204	61	2,940
3	249	75	3,610
4	294	88	4,230
B. REHABILITATION (BC3)			
1	$121	$36	$1,728
2	155	47	2,280
3	190	57	2,736
4	224	67	3,216

* Based on a rent supplement equal to 70% of market rents.

the supplement payment for an average unit each year into the assumed appropriation. Results for both the new construction and rehabilitation projects are shown below and in Graph A–14.

Annual Rent Supplement Appropriations	*Number of New Construction Units Provided*	*Number of Rehabilitation Units Provided*
$10,000,000	5,257	6,896
25,000,000	13,142	17,223
50,000,000	26,285	34,446
75,000,000	39,427	51,669

Step 16: Public Housing Program Applied to Nonprofit Base Cases

Step 16 determines the impact of Public Housing Program subsidies applied to a new construction (nonprofit) project and a rehabilitation (nonprofit) project. The following adjustments are required in the new construction BC:

- Annual interest and amortization payments for the market mortgage with a 6.75% interest rate and a 40-year term equal $161,389. This debt service is fully subsidized.
- Real estate taxes of $24,730 are replaced by a 50% payment in lieu of taxes.
- Vacancy and collection losses are reduced by one-half, from $24,730 to $12,365 per year.

Similar adjustments are made for the rehabilitation BC:

- Annual debt service of $111,299 is fully subsidized.
- Payment in lieu of taxes equals $9,392.
- Vacancy and collection losses of $18,784 are reduced to $9,392.

Table A–23 presents basic rents and minimum income levels resulting under the subsidy formula, calculated by HAM and compared with market rents for both project types. Subsidized rents for the new construction project are 33.1% of unsubsidized rents; for the rehabilitation project, 39.9%. The reduction, considering only the debt service subsidy, is to 37.4% and 43.8% for new construction and rehabilitation, respectively.

The number of new or rehabilitated units possible with various annual appropriations for the Public Housing Program is determined by dividing the debt service subsidy for an average unit each year into the assumed appropriation. (Appropriation levels are increased to reflect greater allocations available under this Program.) Results for both new construction and rehabilitation projects are shown below and in Graph A–15.

Annual Public Housing Appropriations	*Number of New Construction Units Provided*	*Number of Rehabilitation Units Provided*
$ 50,000,000	30,980	44,925
100,000,000	61,960	89,850
150,000,000	92,940	134,775
200,000,000	123,920	179,700
250,000,000	154,900	224,620

TABLE A–23. PUBLIC HOUSING BASIC RENTS AND INCOME LEVELS: NEW CONSTRUCTION AND REHABILITATION, NONPROFIT (BC1 AND BC3)

Number of Bedrooms	*Market Rents (per month)*	*Public Housing Basic Rents (per month)*	*Minimum Income Levels (per year)*
A. NEW CONSTRUCTION (BC1)			
1	$158	$52	$2,536
2	204	67	3,220
3	249	82	3,955
4	294	97	4,672
B. REHABILITATION (BC3)			
1	$121	$48	$2,300
2	155	62	2,962
3	190	75	3,615
4	224	89	4,278

GRAPH A–15. ANNUAL PUBLIC HOUSING APPROPRIATIONS VS. NUMBER OF UNITS PROVIDED: NEW CONSTRUCTION AND REHABILITATION, NONPROFIT (BC1 AND BC3)

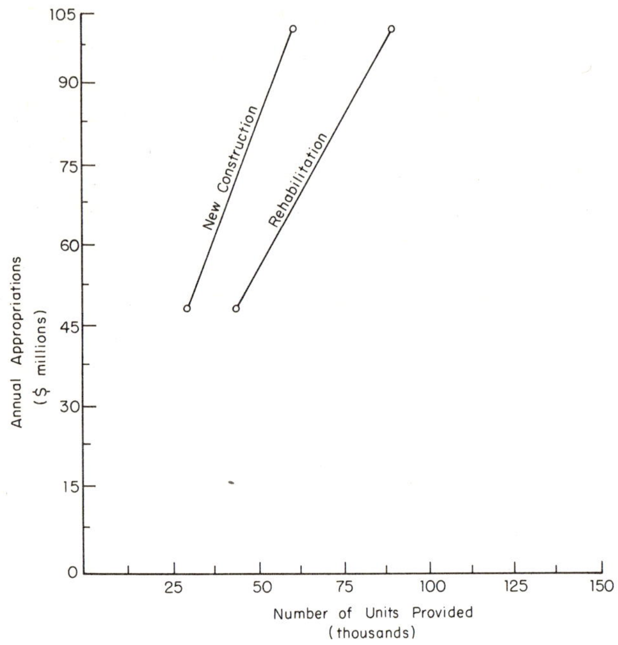

Step 17: Section 506 Program Applied to Nonprofit Base Cases

Step 17 determines the impact of Section 506 subsidies applied to a new construction (nonprofit) project and to a rehabilitation (nonprofit) project, assuming that the land or the land and building acquisition cost is reduced to $1 per unit. Table A–24 presents basic rents and minimum income levels resulting under this subsidy formula, as calculated by HAM and compared with market rents for both BC projects. Subsidized rents for the new construction project are 95.9% of unsubsidized rents. This means a reduction in average rent from $227 to $218 per month. Rehabilitation project rents are reduced to 88.9% of original levels, from $173 to $154 per month.

The number of new or rehabilitated units possible with various annual appropriations for the Section 506 Program is determined by dividing the amount of writedown per unit into the assumed appropriations. Results for both the new construction and rehabilitation projects are shown at the top of the next column and in Graph A–16.

Annual Section 506 Appropriations	*Number of New Construction Units Provided*	*Number of Rehabilitation Units Provided*
$ 5,000,000	5,000	2,500
10,000,000	10,000	5,000
25,000,000	25,000	12,500
50,000,000	50,000	25,000

TABLE A–24. SECTION 506 BASIC RENTS AND INCOME LEVELS: NEW CONSTRUCTION AND REHABILITATION, NONPROFIT (BC1 AND BC3)

Number of Bedrooms	*Market Rents (per month)*	*Section 506 Basic Rents (per month)*	*Minimum Income Levels (per month)*
A. NEW CONSTRUCTION (BC1)			
1	$158	$153	$ 7,326
2	204	196	9,419
3	249	240	11,512
4	294	283	13,605
B. REHABILITATION (BC3)			
1	$121	$108	$ 5,194
2	155	139	6,672
3	190	170	8,160
4	224	201	9,648

GRAPH A–16. ANNUAL SECTION 506 APPROPRIATIONS VS. NUMBER OF NEW UNITS PROVIDED: NEW CONSTRUCTION AND REHABILITATION, NONPROFIT (BC1 AND BC3)

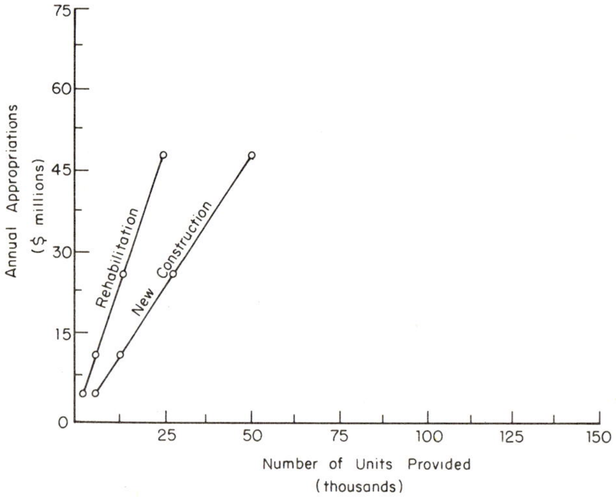

BIBLIOGRAPHY

Abrams, Charles. *Man's Struggle for Shelter in an Urbanizing World.* (Cambridge: MIT Press, 1964.)

__________. *The City is the Frontier.* (New York: Harper & Row, 1965.)

__________. *The Future of Housing.* (New York: Harper & Brothers, 1946.)

Alberts, William W., "Business Cycles, Residential Construction Cycles, and the Mortgage Market," *70 Journal of Political Economy 10* (1962).

Alonso, William. *Location and Land Use: Toward a General Theory of Land Rent.* (Cambridge: Harvard University Press, 1968.)

Andrews, Richard. *Urban Growth and Development.* (New York: Simmons-Boardman, 1962.)

Ash, Jean. "Residential Rehabilitation in the U.S.A.," *3 Urban Studies 22* (1967).

Association of the Bar of the City of New York. Special Committee on the Constitutional Convention, *State Finance, Taxation, and Housing and Community Development* (New York, 1967).

Back, Kurt W. *Slums, Projects, and People.* (Durham, N.C.: Duke University Press, 1959.)

Bailey, Martin J., "Effects of Race and Demographic Factors on the Values of Single-Family Homes," *1 Land Economics 215* (1966).

Banfield, Edward. *Government and Housing in Metropolitan Areas.* (New York: McGraw-Hill, 1958.)

Barlowe, Raleigh. *Land Resource Economics.* (Englewood Cliffs, N.J.: Prentice-Hall, 1958.)

Bartke, Richard W., "The Federal Housing Administration: Its History & Operations," *13 Wayne Law Review 651* (1967).

Bauer, Raymond A. "The Dreary Deadlock of Public Housing," *106 Architectural Forum 140* (1957).

Beyer, Glenn H. *Housing and Society.* (New York: Macmillan, 1965.)

Boston University School of Law, Law and Poverty Project, *The Poor and Public Housing.* (Boston, 1967.)

Brady, Eugene A., "Regional Cycles of Residential Construction and the Interregional Mortgage Market," *1 Land Economics 1* (1963).

__________, "A Sectoral Econometric Study of the Postwar Residential Housing Market," *75 Journal of Political Economy 147* (1967).

Brown, J. Bruce, "Incidence of Property Taxes Under Three Alternative Systems in Urban Areas in New Zealand," *21 National Tax Journal 237* (1968).

"Building Codes, Housing Codes, & the Conservation of Chicago's Housing Supply," *31 University of Chicago Law Review 180* (1963).

Bureau of Community Development, Commonwealth of Pennsylvania. *Financing Lower & Middle Income Housing.* (Philadelphia, 1964.)

Butler, Warren H., "Approach to Low and Moderate Income Home Ownership," *22 Rutgers Law Review 67* (1967).

Calderwood, D. M. *Principles of Mass Housing.* (Pretoria, South Africa: African Council for Scientific and Industrial Research, 1968.)

California, University of, Real Estate Research Program. *Essays in Urban Land Economics* (1966).

Campbell, Burnham O. *Population Change and Building Cycles.* (Urbana: University of Illinois Press, 1966.)

Citizen's Housing and Planning Council of New York. *How Tax Exemption Broke the Housing Deadlock in New York City; A Report of a Study of the Post-World War II Housing Shortage and the Various Efforts to Overcome It* (New York, 1960).

__________. *Tax Policies and Urban Renewal in New York City; A Report on a Tax Study With Recommendations* (New York, 1960).

Clark, Louis M., "The Real Estate Condominium: Its Tax Problems and Implications," *35 The Appraisal Journal 475* (1967).

Colean, Miles L., and Newcomb, R., *Stabilizing Construction: The Record and Potential.* (New York: McGraw-Hill, 1960.)

Colwell, Robert C., "Some Structural Features of U.S. Housing and Home Finance," *21 Federal Bar Journal 447* (1961).

"Conservation and Rehabilitation of Housing: An Idea Approaches Adolescence," *63 University of Michigan Law Review 892* (1965).

"Cooperative Apartments in Government—Assisted Low-Middle Income Housing" *111 University of Pennsylvania Law Review 638* (1963).

Davis, O., "The Economics of Urban Renewal," *26 Journal of Law and Contemporary Problems 1* (1961).

Denton, R. Harold. *Science and Housing.* (Washington: Federal Housing Administration, June 1966.)

Dunhill, Norman, "Diverse Needs and the Role of the Housing Society Movement in Meeting Them," *17 Housing Review 149* (1968).

Dyckman, John W. *Capital Requirements for Urban Development and Renewal.* (New York: McGraw-Hill, 1961.)

"Enforcement of Municipal Housing Codes," *78 Harvard Law Review 801* (1965).

"Federal Aids for Enforcement of Housing Codes," *40 New York University Law Review 948* (1965).

Fisfis, Nick S., and Greenberg, Harold, "Surburban Renewal in Pennsylvania," *111 University of Pennsylvania Law Review 61* (1962).

Fisher, Robert. *Twenty Years of Public Housing.* (New York: Harper, 1959.)

Fitzpatrick, B.T., "FHA & FNMA Assistance for Multi Family Housing" *32 Law and Contemporary Problems 439* (1967).

Foote, Nelson. *Housing Choices and Housing Constraints.* (New York: McGraw-Hill, 1960.)

Freeman, Elsa S., "Review of the Literature on Housing and Urban Development During 1964 & 1965," *57 Special Libraries 156* (1966).

Frieden, Bernard J. "Housing and National Urban Goals: Old Policies and New Realities," in *The Metropolitan Enigma.* (Washington: Chamber of Commerce of the United States, 1967.)

__________. "Locational Preferences in the Urban Housing Market," *27 Journal of the American Institute of Planners 316* (1961).

__________. "Policies for Rebuilding," in *The Future of Old Neighborhoods.* (Cambridge: published for the Joint Center for Urban Studies by the MIT Press, 1964.)

Friedley, Philip, "A Note on the Retail Trade Multiplier and Residential Mobility," *6 Journal of Regional Sciences 1* (1965).

Friedman, L. M. *Government and Slum Housing.* (Chicago: Rand McNally, 1968.)

__________, "Public Housing and the Poor: An Overview," *54 University of California (Berkeley) Law Review 642* (1966).

Friedman, L. M., and Krier, James E., "New Lease on Life: Section 23 Housing and the Poor" *116 University of Pennsylvania Law Review 611* (1968).

Givens, M. B. "Job Security in the Building Industry—And High Quality Low-Rent Housing" *18 Labor Law Journal 468* (1967).

Glazer, Nathan, "Housing Problems and Housing Policies," *7 The Public Interest 21* (1967).

Glazer, Nathan (ed.) *Studies in Housing and Minority Groups.* (Berkeley: University of California Press, 1960.)

Goldston, E., Hunter, A. O., and Rothrauff, G. A., Jr., "Urban Redevelopment—The Viewpoint of Counsel for a Private Redeveloper," *26 Law and Contemporary Problems 118* (1961).

"Government Housing Assistance to the Poor," *76 Yale Law Journal 508* (1967).

"Governmental Programs to Encourage Private Investment in Low-Income Housing," *81 Harvard Law Review 1295* (1968).

Grebler, Leo. *Capital Formation in Residential Real Estate.* (Princeton: Princeton University Press, 1956.)

__________. *Housing Issues in Economic Stabilization Policy.* (New York: National Bureau of Economic Research, Occasional Papers, 72, 1960.)

__________. *Housing Market Behavior in a Declining Area.* (New York: Columbia University Press, 1952.)

Greve, John. *The Housing Problem.* (London: Fabian Society, 1961.)

Gribetz, Judah, and Grad, Frank P., "Housing Code Enforcement: Sanctions & Remedies," *66 Columbia Law Review 1254* (1966).

Grier, E., and Grier, G. *Privately Developed Interracial Housing.* (Berkeley: University of California Press, 1960.)

Grier, Eunice. *Large Family Rent Subsidy Demonstration* Program. (Washington: Government Printing Office, 1966.)

Grigsby, William G. *Housing Markets and Public Policy.* (Philadelphia: University of Pennsylvania Press, 1967.)

Gruen, Claude. *Quality Differences Versus Differentiation in Urban Housing.* (San Francisco: Arthur D. Little, Inc., 1966.)

Guttentag, Jack M., "The Short Cycle in Residential Construction," *61 The American Economic Review* (1961).

Haar, Charles M. *Federal Credit and Private Housing: the Mass Financing Dilemma.* (New York: McGraw-Hill, 1960.)

__________. *Land-Use Planning.* (Boston: Little-Brown, 1959.)

Hagman, Donald G., "Open Space Planning and Property Taxation—Some Suggestions," *University of Wisconsin Law Review 628* (1964).

__________, "Single Tax and Land Use Planning—Henry George Updated" *12 University of California at Los Angeles Law Review 762* (1965).

Heilbrun, James. *Real Estate Taxes and Urban Housing.* (New York: Columbia University Press, 1966.)

Heimann, John G. *The Necessary Revolution in Housing Finance.* (Washington: Urban America, Inc. 1967.)

"Housing: A Symposium," *32 Law and Contemporary Problems, 2, 187* (1967).

"Housing Rehabilitation and the Pittsburgh Graded Property Tax," *2 Duquesne Law Review 213* (1964).

Howorth, H. P., "Site Value Taxation: A Solution to Allocation Problems in the Taxation of Real Estate" *47 Massachusetts Law Quarterly 28* (1962).

Hoyt, Homer. *The Urban Real Estate Cycle—Performances and Prospects* (Washington: Urban Land Institute, Technical Bulletin No. 38, 1960.)

Hunt, William D. *Creative Control of Building Costs.* (New York: McGraw-Hill, 1967.)

Johnson, Don, "Legal Problems of Cooperative Housing in Illinois," *50 Illinois Bar Journal 940* (1962).

Joseph, "Residential Development," *116 New Law Journal 911* (1966).

Kaiser, E. E. *A Decent Home: A Report of the President's Committee on Urban Housing.* (Washington, 1968.)

Kingsbury, Laura M. *The Economics of Housing.* (Morningside Heights, New York: Kings Crown Press, 1946.)

Koch, Carl, "Finally A Low-Cost Component System for Housing That Really Works," *Architectural Record* (March 1967).

Kozol, Lee H., "Massachusetts Fair Housing Practices Land," *47 Massachusetts Law Quarterly 295* (1962).

Krier, James E., "Rent Supplement Program of 1965: Out of the Ghetto Into the . . .?," *19 Stanford Law Review 355* (1967).

Lavrenti, Luigi. *Property Values and Race.* (Berkeley: University of California Press, 1960.)

Ledbetter, William H., Jr., "Public Housing—A Social Experiment Seeks Acceptance," *32 Law and Contemporary Problems 490* (1967).

Lefcoe, G., "Monetary Corrections and Mortgage Lending in Brazil: Observations for the United States," *21 Stanford Law Review 106* (1968).

Levi, Julian H., "Focal Leverage Points in Problems Relating to Real Property," *66 Columbia Law Review* 275 (1966).

Lindauer, Smigh, "Effects of the Punjab Land Tax," *19 National Tax Journal 427* (1966).

Little, Arthur D., Inc. *Model of San Francisco Housing Market.* (San Francisco: Community Renewal Program, 1966.)

Lubove, Roy. *The Urban Community.* (Englewood Cliffs: Prentice Hall, 1967.)

Maisel, Sherman, "The Economic Aspects of Housing," in *The International Encyclopedia of Social Sciences.* (New York: Crowell, Collier & MacMillan, 1968.)

__________. *Housebuilding in Transition.* (Berkeley: University of California Press, 1953.)

__________, "Fluctuations in Residential Construction Starts" *53 American Economic Review* (1963).

Maisel, Sherman, and Grebler, Leo, "Determinants of Residential Construction: A Review of Present Knowledge," in *Impacts of Monetary Policy.* (Englewood Cliffs: Prentice Hall, 1963.)

Mandelker, Daniel. *Managing Our Urban Environments.* (Indianapolis, Indiana: Bobbs-Merrill Company, 1966.)

Massachusetts. Legislative Research Council. *Report Submitted by the Legislative Research Council on Relating Massachusetts and Federal Public Housing Laws.* (Boston, 1959.)

__________, Special Commission Established to Make an Investigation and Study Relative to Housing for Families and Individuals of Low Income. *Report.* (Boston, 1965.)

__________, Special Commission on Low Income Housing. *Final Report.* (Boston, 1965.)

McCormack, James E., "Appraisal of Urban Renewal Property for Moderate Income Low-Rent Public Housing" *35 The Appraisal Journal 71* (1967).

Meyerson, Martin, Terrett, B., and Wheaton, W. L. *Housing, People, and Cities.* (New York: McGraw-Hill, 1962.)

Mills, Edwin S., "An Aggregative Model of Resource Allocation in a Metropolitan Area," *57 American Economic Review 1* (1967).

Mulvihill, Roger, "Problems in the Managment of Public Housing" *35 Temple Law Quarterly 163* (1962).

Muth, Richard, "Slums and Poverty" in Nevitt, Adela (ed.), *The Economic Problems of Housing.* (New York: Macmillan 1967.)

__________, "The Demand for Non-Farm Housing" in Harberger, A. C. (ed.). *The Demand for Durable Goods.* (Chicago: University of Chicago Press, 1960.)

National Association of Home Builders. *Annual List of Periodical Articles* (1967).

__________. *Building Codes: A List of References* (1960).

National Association of Housing and Redevelopment Officials. *The Constitutionality of Housing Codes* (1961).

__________. *Critical Housing Issues: 1967* (1967).

Netzer, Dick. *Economics of the Property Tax.* (Washington: Brookings Institution, 1966.)

New Housing Panel. *A Report of the New Housing Panel.* (Woods Hole, Massachusetts: Summer Study on Science and Urban Development, June 5–25, 1966.)

__________. *Background and Summary, Report of the New Housing Panel.* (Woods Hole, Massachusetts: Summer Study on Science and Urban Development, June 5–25, 1966.)

Nevitt, Adela. *Housing, Taxation and Subsidies: A Study of Housing in the United Kingdom.* (London: Nelson, 1966.)

__________. *The Economic Problems of Housing.* (New York: Macmillan, 1967.)

New York (State) Executive Department; Division of Housing. *Housing Codes: The Key to Housing Conservation.* (1960; 3 v.)

Nimmo, James Ferguson, "Commonwealth Home Savings Grant and Housing Loans Insurance Schemes," *39 Law Institute Journal 17* (1965).

Ontario Department of Municipal Affairs. *Housing Code Program: A Summary of Experience on Selected American Communities* (1961).

Orr, Larry L., "Incidence of Differential Property Tax on Urban Housing," *21 National Tax Journal 253* (1968).

Pickard, Jerome. *Urban Real Estate Research, 1963.* (Washington: Urban Land Institute, 1965.)

"Preference Liens for the Cost of Repairing Slum Property," *19 Washington University Land Quarterly 141* (1967).

Princeton University, Conference No. 88. *Cooperation of the Public and Private Sectors in Housing* (1968).

Quirk, William J., Wein, Leon E., and Gomberg, Ira, "A Draft Program of Housing Reform—The Tenant Condominium," *53 Cornell Law Review 361* (1968).

Rapkin, Chester, and Grigsby, William G. *Residential Renewal in the Urban Core.* (Philadelphia: University of Pennsylvania Press, 1960.)

Rawson, Mary. *Property Taxation & Urban Development.* (Washington: Urban Land Institute, 1961.)

Reid, Margaret. *Housing and Income.* (Chicago: University of Chicago Press, 1962.)

"Rent Withholding and the Improvement of Substandard Housing," *53 University of California (Berkeley) Law Review 304* (1965).

Robinson, Herbert W. *The Economics of Building.* (London: P. S. King & Son, Ltd., 1939.)

Rodwin, Lloyd. *Housing and Economic Progress; A Study of Housing Experiences of Boston's Middle-*

Income Families. (Cambridge: Harvard University Press, 1961.)

Ross, William B., "A Proposed Methodology for Comparing Federal Assisted Housing Programs," *57 American Economic Review 91* (1967).

Rothenberg, J. "Urban Renewal Programs," in Dorfman, R. (ed.) *Measuring Benefits of Government Investments.* (Washington: Brookings Institution, 1965.)

Scheele, D. Sam, "Urban Housing: An Apologetic for a Radical Mechanism to Promote Initiative and Excellence," *45 Journal of Urban Law 347* (1967).

Schorr, Alvin. *Slums and Social Insecurity: An Appraisal of the Effectiveness of Housing Policies in Helping to Eliminate Poverty in the United States.* (Washington: U.S. Department of Health, Education and Welfare, 1963.)

Shelton, John P., "The Cost of Renting Versus Owning a Home," *2 Land Economics 59* (1968).

Singer, Bruce S., "A Systematic Approach to Housing Market Analysis," *35 The Appraisal Journal 527* (1967).

Smolensky, Eugene, "Public Housing or Income Supplements—The Economics of Housing for the Poor," *The Journal of the American Institute of Planners 94* (1968).

Sport, A., "Empirical Studies in the Economics of Slum Ownership," *36 Land Economics 340* (1960).

Sternlieb, George, "Household Research in the Urban Core," *32 Journal of Marketing 25* (1968).

__________. *The Tenement Landlord.* (New Brunswick, New Jersey: The William Byrd Press, 1966.)

"Symposium: New Directions in Land Use Control—Housing & Urban Development," *1965 ABA Section on Real Property Law 4* (1965).

"Symposium on Housing & Home Finance," *10 New York Law Forum 459* (1964).

"Symposium on Housing & Home Finance," *11 New York Law Forum 1* (1965).

"Tenants and Rent Strikes," *3 Columbia Journal of Law and Social Problems 1* (1967).

"Toward Optimal Land Use: Property Tax Policy and Land Use Planning," *53 University of California Law Review 856* (1967).

Tweed, R. B., "Improvement of Older Houses," *117 New Law Journal 205* (1967).

U.S. Commission on Civil Rights. *Massachusetts Advisory Committee: Discrimination in Housing in the Boston Metropolitan Area.* (Washington, 1963.)

__________. *Massachusetts Advisory Committee—Report on Massachusetts: Housing Discrimination in the Springfield-Holyoke-Chicopee Metropolitan Area.* (Washington, 1966.)

U.S. Commission on Money and Credit, *Impacts on Monetary Policy.* (Washington, 1964.)

U.S. Department of Housing & Urban Development. *Administration of a Systematic Housing Code Compliance Program* (1967).

__________. *Bibliography on Housing, Building, and Planning* (1966).

__________. *Housing and Urban Development Trends* (1968).

__________. *Rehabilitation Programs: A Report to the Subcommittee on Housing and Urban Affairs of the Senate Committee on Banking and Currency* (1967).

__________. *The Rent Supplement Program for Low Income Families* (1967).

U.S. General Accounting Office. *Review of Policies & Procedures for Controlling and Sharing the Costs of Slum Clearance and Urban Renewal Projects* (1962).

U.S. House of Representatives, Banking and Currency Committee. *Basic Laws and Authorities on Housing, and Urban Development, Revised through Jan. 15, 1968* (1968).

__________. *Summary of the Housing and Urban Development Act of 1968* (1968).

U.S. Housing and Home Finance Agency. *Addresses by Robert C. Weaver and Others* (1963).

__________. *Housing for Senior Citizens* (1962).

__________. *Low Income Housing Demonstration . . . A Search for Solutions* (1964).

__________. *State Enabling Legislation, List of Citations to Statutes, Constitutional Provisions, and Court Decisions* (1962).

__________. *Urban Expansion Problems and Needs* (1963).

U.S. National Committee on Technology, Automation, & Economic Progress, *Applying Technology to Unmet Needs* (1966).

U.S. Office of Economic Opportunity. *Community Action and Urban Housing* (1967).

U.S. Senate, Committee on Government Operations Subcommittee on Intergovernmental Relations. *Criteria for Evaluation in Planning State and Local Programs* (1967).

U.S. Senate, Subcommittee on Housing, Committee on Banking and Currency. *Study of Mortgage Credit* (1967).

Urban Land Institute. *New Approaches to Residential Land Development.* (Washington: Technical Bulletin No. 40, 1961.)

__________. *The Home Association Handbook.* (Washington, 1966.)

__________. *Urban Real Estate Research.* (Washington, 1959– .)

Weinstein, Lewis H., "Urban Renewal in Massachusetts," *47 Massachusetts Law Quarterly 5* (1962).

Wendt, Paul F. *Housing Policy—The Search for Solutions.* (Berkeley: University of California Press, 1962.)

Wheaton, William L. *Urban Housing.* (New York: Free Press, 1966.)

Winnick, L. *Rental Housing Opportunities for Private Investment.* (New York: McGraw-Hill, 1958.)

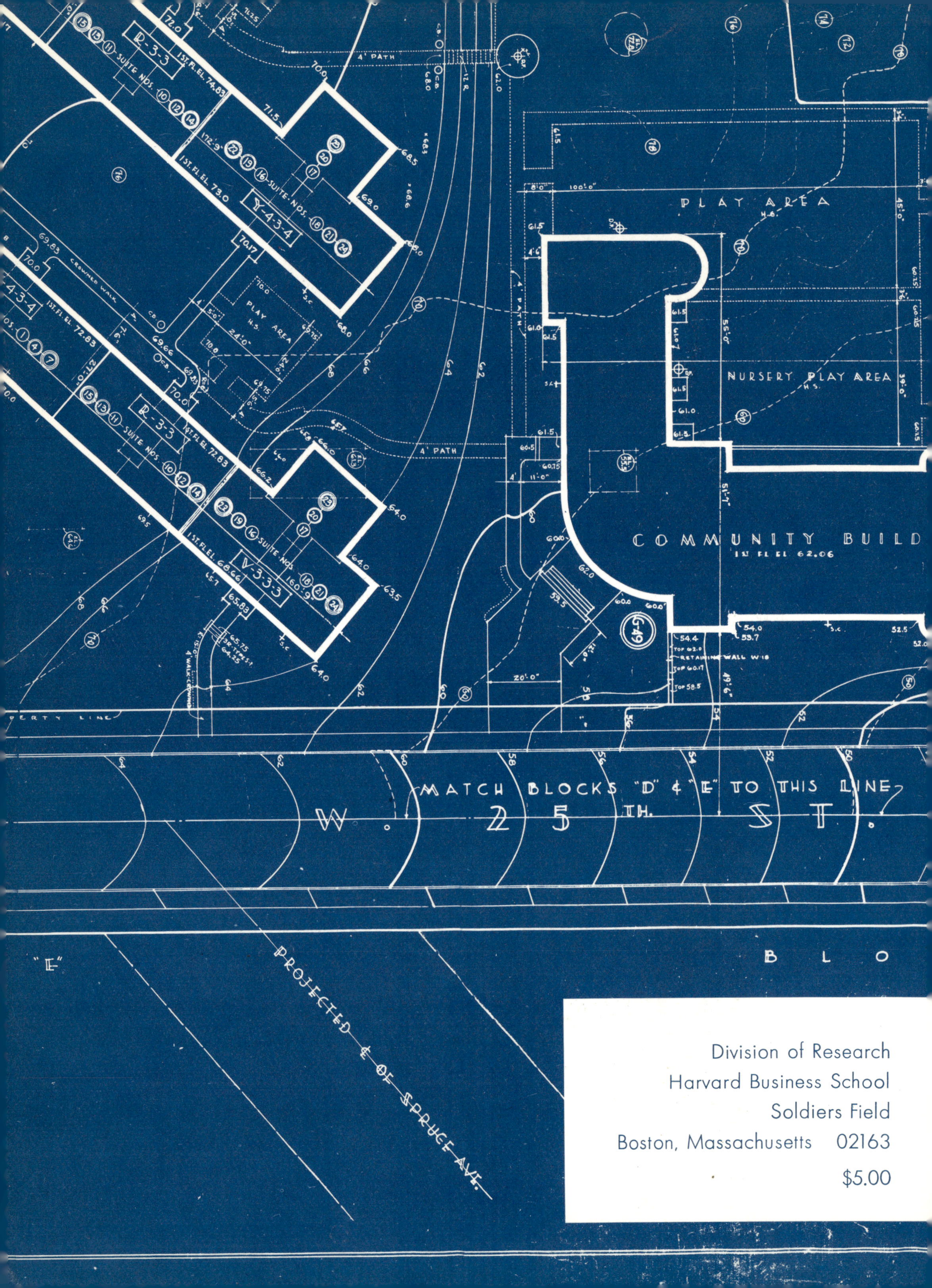

Division of Research
Harvard Business School
Soldiers Field
Boston, Massachusetts 02163

$5.00